# DATE DUE

| | | | |
|---|---|---|---|
| SEP 0 9 2009 | | | |
| | | | |
| | | | |
| | | | |
| | | | |
| | | | |
| | | | |
| | | | |
| | | | |
| | | | |
| | | | |
| | | | |
| | | | |
| | | | |
| | | | |

*The Southern Journey of a Civil War Marine*

NUMBER TEN

*Clifton and Shirley Caldwell Texas Heritage Series*

# The Southern Journey
# of a Civil War Marine

## THE ILLUSTRATED NOTE-BOOK
## OF HENRY O. GUSLEY

*Edited and Annotated by Edward T. Cotham, Jr.*

UNIVERSITY OF TEXAS PRESS *Austin*

*Publication of this work was made possible in part by support from Clifton and Shirley Caldwell and a challenge grant from the National Endowment for the Humanities.*

*Requests for permission to reproduce material
from this work should be sent to:*
    Permissions
    University of Texas Press
    P.O. Box 7819, Austin, TX 78713-7819
    www.utexas.edu/utpress/about/bpermission.html

∞ The paper used in this book meets the minimum requirements of ANSI/NISO Z39.48-1992 (R1997) (Permanence of Paper).

LIBRARY OF CONGRESS CATALOGING-IN-PUBLICATION DATA

Gusley, Henry O., 1837–1884. The Southern journey of a Civil War marine : the illustrated note-book of Henry O. Gusley / edited and annotated by Edward T. Cotham, Jr.—1st ed.
        p.        cm.—(Clifton and Shirley Caldwell Texas heritage series ; no. 10)
Includes index.
ISBN 0-292-71283-9 (cloth : alk. paper)
1. United States—History—Civil War, 1861–1865—Naval operations.
2. Gulf Coast (U.S.)—History, Naval—19th century.   3. Gulf States—History,
Military—19th century.   4. Mexico, Gulf of—History, Naval—19th century.
5. Gusley, Henry O., 1837–1884—Diaries.   6. United States—History—Civil
War, 1861–1865—Personal narratives.   7. United States. Marine Corps—
Biography.   8. Seafaring life—Gulf Coast (U.S.)—History—19th century.
9. United States. Marine Corps—Military life—History—19th century.
10. Gulf Coast (U.S.)—Description and travel.   I. Cotham, Edward T.
(Edward Terrel), 1953– II. Title.   III. Series.
E591.G87 2006
973.7'58—dc22

                                                                2005027611

*Book & jacket design by Michael S. Williams*

This book is dedicated to Ann Caraway Ivins and William D. Quick

# Contents

# Acknowledgments

Tʜɪs book has its origin in a remarkable coincidence. In 1999 my friend Harry Bounds mentioned to me that he had run across some unusual drawings in the Special Collections of the Nimitz Library at the U.S. Naval Academy. Harry had found these drawings particularly interesting because they included depictions of the Battle of Galveston, a local battle of mutual interest that had been the subject of a book I had written in 1998.

In looking over the list of drawings that Harry had discovered in the Naval Academy's collection, I was amazed to discover the existence of more than eighty sketches by Dr. Daniel D. T. Nestell, most of them depicting battles in which the Union gunboat U.S.S. *Clifton* had taken part. These drawings were of more than passing interest to me since I was then in the process of writing a book about the Battle of Sabine Pass, the battle at which *Clifton* was captured in 1863. I made plans to use some of the Nestell drawings in my Sabine Pass book and put away the list of the remaining drawings in a file. Something about the drawings, however, continued to nag at the edges of my memory.

Several years later, I happened to open a file of copied newspaper articles that I had put together while researching my book on Civil War Galveston. In scanning the contents of the folder, I came across a lengthy excerpt copied from various fall 1863 issues of the *Galveston Tri-Weekly News*. It was the "Note-Book" (as the newspaper called it) of Henry O. Gusley, a U.S. Marine who had been captured at the Battle of Sabine Pass while serving in the Marine Guard on *Clifton*. As I began looking at the events recorded in the Note-Book, I noticed a remarkable and exciting similarity between the events described in Gusley's Note-Book and the drawings Harry Bounds had come across in the Naval Academy's collection.

The more I studied the two collections, the more similarities I detected. Where the narrative in Gusley's Note-Book described a waterspout, I found that Nestell's drawings depicted one. I decided to see if the reverse was also true. I noticed that one of Nestell's drawings showed an alligator on the Pearl River. When I then looked up the corresponding entry for the same date in Gusley's Note-Book, I was delighted to see that Gusley recorded seeing exactly the same creature. It quickly became apparent to me that what I had stumbled across was in essence the sound track that went with a virtual slide show of the Civil War up and down the Mississippi and all along the Gulf Coast.

It was evident from the outset of this project that the Note-Book and the drawings illustrating it involved Civil War places and events far outside Texas, the subject of my previous research. Fortunately, I was able to enlist the help of some extremely competent historians who specialized in these other areas. I want to particularly acknowledge the assistance of David Sullivan, the leading expert on the subject of the U.S. Marines in the Civil War, who read this manuscript and offered many helpful comments and corrections. Art Bergeron, an expert on wartime Mobile and Louisiana (among many other things), was also kind enough to read my manuscript and offer his valuable comments.

Several archives and libraries provided important assistance in connection with this project. Dr. Jennifer A. Bryan, who serves as head of the Special Collections & Archives Division of the Nimitz Library, U.S. Naval Academy, was very helpful in allowing me access to the Nestell collection and granting permission to publish the Nestell drawings. I also received significant help and assistance from the Marine Corps Historical Center, Marine Corps Air-Ground Museum, and the Lancaster County, Pennsylvania, Historical Center. Casey E. Greene, head of the Special Collections of the Galveston and Texas History Center, Rosenberg Library, also provided valuable assistance with research and photographs.

As explained above, Harry Bounds deserves much credit for his role in originating this project. He also assisted by reviewing the manuscript. William D. Quick, of Nederland, Texas, a great friend and inspiration to me, also was tremendously helpful and supportive with this project. I would also like to thank my assistant, Barbie Tyler. Finally, I would like to thank my wife, Candace, without whose help and support this book would not have been possible.

# Introduction

O N September 28, 1863, an unusual item made its first appearance in the *Galveston Tri-Weekly News*. By this time, midway through the Civil War, the Galveston newspaper was actually being published in Houston, where most of its regular readers had fled from the coast to escape the threat of Union blockade and bombardment. These transplanted readers opened their papers to see featured on page 1 the beginning installment of what was referred to in a large headline as "A Yankee Note-Book." This "Note-Book," covering more than 150 pages and eighteen months of time, was in reality a journal that had been seized by Confederate authorities from a U.S. Marine captured on September 8, 1863, after the Battle of Sabine Pass.

Over the course of almost two months, the readers of the *News*, then one of the most influential newspapers in the South, were treated to the full contents of Henry O. Gusley's remarkable narrative. This diary, or "Note-Book" as Gusley described it in the published version, recorded the private thoughts and experiences of one very articulate and witty Marine. Never intended for general publication, Gusley's journal was originally created only as a convenient way for the Pennsylvania Marine to record his wartime experiences for the future amusement of his friends and family. He had no idea that his writings would eventually be front-page material in an enemy newspaper. The Note-Book covered an eventful period in its author's life. During the period chronicled in his Note-Book, Gusley took part in a series of military operations up and down the Mississippi River and all along the Gulf Coast from Florida to Texas. These battles included large engagements at New Orleans and Vicksburg, as well as smaller conflicts in the coastal waters of Louisiana and Texas.

The Yankee Note-Book quickly became one of the most popular

sections in the Galveston newspaper. To promote this unexpectedly popular feature, the *News* chose to publish Gusley's Note-Book in serial fashion, tantalizing its readers with excerpts that usually covered no more than one to two months at a time. It quickly became the talk of the town. After the first installment, eager readers demanded that the Note-Book's contents be published at least twice on succeeding days so that they would not miss a word of Gusley's experiences. Thus, for example, the young Marine's journal for the period May 4–5, 1862, was published in the *Tri-Weekly News* both on September 29, 1863, and again the following day.[1]

To his enthusiastic Texas readers in 1863, Gusley's narrative was something of a revelation. Here, for all to read in the newspaper, were nothing less than the candid observations of an enemy. But reading these private reflections was more than an exercise of voyeurism. Contrary to the initial expectations of his Texas readers, the Note-Book's author did not sound much like an enemy. In fact, the private views Gusley expressed in his journal on subjects ranging all the way from slavery to the Lincoln Administration were not much different from those of his new Confederate audience. On many occasions the Note-Book read more like a simple travelogue or a study of poetry and literature. It was certainly nothing like the inflammatory rhetoric that was a common feature in most Northern speeches inserted in Southern newspapers to stoke the fires of secession. The Note-Book also failed to meet some readers' preconceptions inasmuch as it was not the ravings of a fanatical abolitionist, as many Texans would have expected. Instead, what gradually emerged in the pages of the "Yankee Note-Book" was a literate, candid, and often humorous examination of the war as seen through the eyes of one very small cog in the immense Union war machine.

At first, the identity of the Note-Book's author was kept a mystery from its readers, ostensibly because the *News* feared that publication of its writer's name might "operate prejudicially to the author." It was not clear whether this prejudice was feared to come from Southerners, Northerners, or literary critics. But in any event, the anonymous status of the Note-Book's author soon changed when Gusley wrote a letter to the newspaper from his place of confinement at Camp Groce near Hempstead, enclosing five dollars and asking for copies of all of the issues in which his narrative was printed. The Galveston newspaper complied with this remarkable subscription request and an unusual public and published correspondence then followed between the prisoner-turned-celebrity and Willard Richardson, the editor of the newspaper.

As preserved so fortunately in the pages of Richardson's newspaper, Gusley's Note-Book contains many wonderful and historically valuable descriptions of important military events. Perhaps even more significant, however, are the Note-Book's vivid descriptions of ordinary daily life on board two active Union warships. For these reasons, the preservation of Gusley's journal in the pages of a Texas newspaper was indeed a remarkable stroke of luck for modern historians. But in an even more remarkable coincidence, in addition to Gusley's narrative, a number of remarkably detailed sketches have been independently preserved that provide a visual representation of many of the same places and events that Gusley visited and witnessed. These sketches have survived because yet another Union participant in a nearby ship (a ship to which Gusley himself was eventually transferred) felt the same compulsion that Gusley did to record his wartime experiences and environment in a tangible form.

Dr. Daniel D. T. Nestell, who served as Acting Assistant Surgeon on board the steamer *Clifton*, was (like Gusley) a keen observer of life aboard ship in the West Gulf Blockading Squadron. What Gusley preserved in words, Dr. Nestell preserved in his drawings. As the reader will soon recognize in these pages, Nestell was quite talented as a sketch artist. We are indeed fortunate that more than eighty of his sketches are today preserved in the Special Collections of the Nimitz Library of the U.S. Naval Academy in Annapolis, Maryland. Combined here for the first time, Gusley's words published in a Texas newspaper and Nestell's pictures preserved at the Naval Academy together provide an unequaled glimpse into the U.S. Navy's campaigns along the Mississippi River and the Gulf Coast.

In many ways, the written and pictorial descriptions that Gusley and Nestell produced serve the same function as if they had jointly written a series of picture postcards home from the war they experienced. Together, they document some spectacular Union successes (like the capture of New Orleans) as well as some of the most embarrassing incidents (like the Confederate victories at Galveston and Sabine Pass) in the U.S. Navy's long history. They also provide some fascinating and unique glimpses into everyday life in the naval forces operating along the Gulf Coast ("Uncle Sam's nephews in the Gulf" as Gusley affectionately referred to them).

Gusley's words and Nestell's drawings serve to provide a valuable record of the conflict that so divided and yet in a strange way served to unite the states that today comprise America. That may ultimately be the most important value that publication of Gusley's diary served. The Texans who read the pages of the young Marine's diary in the newspaper during the fall of 1863 must have been struck with the same impression that we have reading it today. Gusley comes across as a person to whom almost anyone could relate, a man whom it would be easy to call a friend. Changing enemies into friends would, of course, not be an overnight transformation. But reading Gusley's narrative perhaps may have begun the transition process through which his Texas readers would eventually come to regard former enemies like Henry Gusley as fellow countrymen.

## About Henry O. Gusley

Henry O. Gusley was born in Lancaster, Pennsylvania, on November 26, 1837.[2] His father, Jacob Gusley, was one of the hardest-working bricklayers in the city. In fact, on the occasion of Jacob's death in 1880 at the age of 69, the Lancaster newspaper reported that the elder Gusley had "built or assisted in building more of the principal buildings in this city . . . than any other bricklayer in the city."[3] Henry Gusley, however, chose not to follow in his father's construction-oriented footsteps. Perhaps it was the influence of his mother, Elizabeth, but Henry at an early age developed what must have been an unquenchable thirst for poetry, literature, and philosophy. An incredibly well-read young man (as evidenced by the numerous and lengthy literary references and quotations in his Note-Book), Henry eventually decided to turn his passion for the written word into a career. He became a printer, a profession that evidently encouraged its practitioners to become creative, witty, and articulate. Another Pennsylvania printer, Benjamin Franklin, set the standard by which Pennsylvanians like Gusley measured themselves.

Gusley would practice the printing profession in Lancaster only for a few years until the Civil War intervened. When the war broke out, Gusley determined to fight for the Union. At the age of twenty-four, he went to Philadelphia and enlisted in the U.S. Marine Corps for a term of four years. His service began officially with his enlistment on October 11, 1861. Although no photograph of Gusley has yet come to light, the enlistment records reflect that the new Marine was five feet and seven inches in height and had hazel eyes, brown hair, and a fair complexion.

After a brief period of training at Marine Barracks, Washington, D.C., and Brooklyn, New York, Gusley was ordered to join the Marine detachment on U.S.S. *Westfield*. He and his ship left New York on February 22, 1862, after being assigned to service in the Gulf

of Mexico. *Westfield* would find its first service in connection with
the steamer division of the Mortar Flotilla then being assembled for
operations at the mouth of the Mississippi River.

Because of storms and a series of resulting mechanical problems,
Gusley did not actually arrive at the entrance to the Mississippi
until almost a month after his departure from New York. He then
began a period of almost two years of active service in Commodore
(later Admiral) David Glasgow Farragut's West Gulf Blockading
Squadron. During this eventful period, Gusley would find himself
transferred unexpectedly from U.S.S. *Westfield* to another steamer,
U.S.S. *Clifton*, after *Westfield*'s destruction in action. Gusley's ships
were engaged in a series of battles and skirmishes up and down the
Mississippi River. They also played an important role supporting
the U.S. Army in the Teche campaigns in Louisiana.

Gusley's ships participated as well in blockading operations
stretching from Matagorda Bay in Texas all along the Gulf Coast
to Pensacola, Florida. As part of these blockading duties, Gusley
and his shipmates were involved in battles at Galveston, Port Lavaca,
and Sabine Pass. At the conclusion of the Battle of Sabine Pass, one
of the most remarkable Confederate victories of the war, Gusley was
captured. He was thereafter held as a prisoner of war at Camp Groce
(near Hempstead, Texas) and elsewhere in Texas and Louisiana.

Although Gusley's Note-Book records his service in five states,
its descriptions of the war in Texas are particularly valuable since
they vividly point out the divisions that existed among that state's
citizens regarding the war. The Note-Book records, in Gusley's
inimitable style, that at Matagorda the inhabitants "refused to sell
a morsel of anything to a Union man." At Galveston, however, the
Unionist townspeople greeted the Federal fleet with such a warm
reception that Gusley declared that "a more respectable and well
behaved set [of people] we have never seen." Even when he was
captured, Gusley insisted that he found his Texas captors to be
"a polite and generous people."[4]

Perhaps the most interesting features in Gusley's Note-Book are
the incredible powers of study and description that he brings to even
the most routine events aboard ship. Recording a typical Sunday at
sea, for example, Gusley admits to having a "sublime feeling," noting
that the presence of water all around him induced a "deeper feeling
of the beauty and solemnity of the day." At times, Gusley's Note-Book
almost lapses into poetry. Thus, on one sunny day, Gusley observes
that "with a clear bright sky above you and the gently swelling waters
of the Gulf beneath . . . one cannot help feeling happy, even though

he be on an errand of rude war." This is in sharp contrast to his description of a dismal, wet day. On such a day, Gusley observes, "everybody is too wet to talk in a good humor, and so they growl; everything is too damp to admit of a snooze, and that causes everyone to grumble; and so the hours drag along, each seeming in itself a watch, and the day itself seems like an age."[5]

Gusley's nineteen-month period of confinement must indeed have seemed like an "age." The young Marine was not released from captivity until April 1865, when he was paroled. This lengthy period of confinement had been hard on Gusley. He developed a serious stomach disorder, diagnosed later as everything from cancer to chronic peritonitis. This condition afflicted him for the remainder of his life. Causing him incredible pain that literally doubled him over from time to time, this stomach problem frequently prevented him from eating regular meals and kept him from engaging in full-time work after the war. It eventually was the cause of his death in Rochester, New York, on December 19, 1884, at the age of forty-seven.[6]

The original of Gusley's Note-Book does not appear to have survived. We are indeed fortunate, therefore, to have the version that was transcribed so faithfully in the Galveston newspaper. It must be recognized, however, that the editor who rendered Gusley's handwritten Note-Book into newspaper print in 1863 was not as familiar as we are today with the names of Union ships and personnel. In addition, Gusley used a style of punctuation and printer's abbreviations that were apparently difficult to read and reproduce. To minimize these difficulties, in editing Gusley's Note-Book for publication in this book, official records and other sources have been used to revise and occasionally correct the text published in the Galveston newspaper in order to more closely approximate Gusley's meaning and intent. Where it appears that the original text of Gusley's Note-Book (as opposed to the version transcribed in the newspaper) was incomplete or erroneous, and not a mere transcription error, the error is preserved herein. All other changes or corrections have been identified in brackets or otherwise noted.

## About Dr. Daniel D. T. Nestell

The artist behind most of the sketches in this book, Dr. Daniel D. T. Nestell (Figure 1),[7] was born in New York in 1819, making him eighteen years older than Henry Gusley. Nestell attended the City University of New York, where he graduated with a medical degree in 1843. Following graduation, Nestell toured internationally with

FIGURE 1. Dr. Daniel D. T. Nestell. Courtesy of the Nimitz Library, U.S. Naval Academy, Annapolis, Maryland.

one of his medical school professors. During this period he developed an expertise in dispensing medicines as well as becoming a specialist in diagnosing pulmonary ailments.[8]

When the Civil War broke out, Nestell tendered his services as a physician. He was appointed Acting Assistant Surgeon, U.S. Navy, on January 25, 1862. Nestell was first assigned to duty on U.S.S. *Clifton*, on which he served until its capture at the Battle of Sabine Pass on September 8, 1863.

After his capture at Sabine Pass, Dr. Nestell was at first confined with Henry Gusley and the other prisoners from that battle at Camp Groce, near Hempstead, Texas. Eventually most of the officers were moved to Camp Ford, near Tyler, Texas. Dr. Nestell applied for release on the ground that as a physician he was entitled under the accepted rules of war to free passage through the enemy's lines. This request was granted and he was released in the spring of 1864. During his captivity, Dr. Nestell contracted scurvy and lost many of his teeth. After he was released, Nestell was then assigned to serve on board the side-wheel steamer U.S.S. *Alabama*, which had been recommissioned in May 1864. He served as *Alabama*'s physician for the remainder of the war.

This would not turn out to be a quiet period of reflection. *Alabama* was one of the ships assigned to participate in two massive bombardments of Fort Fisher on the North Carolina coast.[9] Nestell, of course, was no stranger to such bombardments, having been present on *Clifton* during many similar attacks beginning with the almost weeklong assault on the forts below New Orleans in the spring of 1862. By the end of the war, Dr. Nestell had endured almost four years on board ships that were active participants in heavy bombardments lasting many days at a time. It is not surprising that this type of service eventually caused Nestell to lose much of his hearing, a condition that continued to worsen after the war.

The end of the war brought personal conflict for Dr. Nestell when he was formally accused by his former commanding officer (Lieutenant Frederick Crocker, U.S.N.) of acting negligently during the Battle of Sabine Pass.[10] This allegation, which did not surface until almost two years after the battle, was delayed because Crocker (unlike Dr. Nestell) was not released from Southern prisons until 1865. When he was eventually confronted with his commander's accusations, Nestell admitted one charge—that he had hidden on his ship's rudder during part of the battle—but denied the more serious allegation that he had failed to care for the wounded to the best of his ability.[11] As it did with many such controversies at the end of the war, the Navy decided simply to sweep these allegations under the rug, and Dr. Nestell's appointment as Acting Assistant Surgeon was simply revoked without comment on June 6, 1865.[12]

After the war ended, Nestell attempted to resume his medical practice, but his growing deafness made it difficult for him to attract and retain private patients. In 1869 Nestell became an Acting Assistant Surgeon with the U.S. Army in Portland, Oregon. Until his retirement in 1874, he continued to serve as an Army physician at various camps and forts in California, Oregon, and Arizona. Nestell died at the age of eighty-one in Oakland, California, on October 24, 1900. His cause of death was officially listed as "senility." He was buried in Mountain View Cemetery.

## About the United States Marine Corps in the Civil War

Today, the United States Marine Corps is a legendary fighting force with proud traditions, an established identity, and a well-defined mission. That was not the case at the time of the Civil War. Although the Marine Corps had been in existence since 1775, when it was created by the Continental Congress, and had seen action on shore

FIGURE 2. Sailors and Marine (Seated Left of Board Game) on the Deck of the U.S. Gunboat *Miami*. National Archives and Records Administration.

in battles ranging from the Mexican War ("the halls of Montezuma") to actions against the Barbary pirates ("the shores of Tripoli"), those actions were only a distant memory for the relatively small number of men who comprised the Marine Corps when the Civil War erupted in 1861.

Before the war was even in progress, the Corps lost a small number of enlisted men and fully one-third of its officers to the ranks of the Confederacy, leaving a depleted service unequipped and unprepared to meet the growing needs of the expanding Union naval forces. To meet these needs, Congress authorized the expansion of the Marine Corps to more than three thousand enlisted men. Henry Gusley was part of this wartime increase in the ranks of the Marines. Although the Marines now had the few good men for whom they were suddenly looking (Figure 2), there was still substantial confusion and uncertainty about the specific role that these new Marines would be expected to play in the rapidly escalating conflict. During the first few months of the war, the Marines served effectively in a number of important actions on land, taking an active role in the fighting at Bull Run and Hatteras Inlet. But as the war progressed,

Marines were assigned less and less of a role on shore, leading to some ambiguity about their function in the Union military machine.

Michael S. Davis accurately summarizes the problem as one of scope:

> The American Civil War demonstrated that Marines had no consistent role in battle. Many fought aboard ships as gun crews and as sharpshooters. Only in a few isolated instances did the Marines fight on land, and then only in small numbers. . . . The Marine Corps' position was that its purpose remained what it had always been: to furnish ship's guards for naval vessels, to enforce shipboard discipline, operate the guns, and join landing parties for very limited operations ashore. . . . Thus, the Marine Corps failed to find a wartime function for itself, a failure that threatened its very existence.[13]

Calling this period the "Doldrums of the Marine Corps," historian Allan R. Millett noted that "The Marine Corps began the Civil War on the defensive both tactically and institutionally, and it never recovered."[14] Marines like Henry Gusley were detached ashore only on limited occasions and usually with very limited objectives. The military planners in Washington had not yet realized the critical importance of having a specially trained force dedicated to making amphibious assaults on enemy positions.

As Gusley's experience points out, life on a naval warship (even a relatively active ship) was seldom glamorous, particularly during the seemingly endless months of routine blockade duty. Like their counterparts on land, Marines frequently complained about boredom and the monotony of their rations. George Riddell, who (like Gusley) was a Marine from Pennsylvania, wrote home to his family to describe the daily menu on board *Clifton*:

Monday—Pork & Beans
Tuesday—Salt Horse [salted beef] & Duff [flour pudding]
Wednesday—Pork & Beans & Pickles
Thursday—Preserved Roast Beef, Desiccated Potatoes, Butter
Friday—Pork & Beans & Pickles
Saturday—Salt Horse & Duff
Sunday—Preserved Meat, Rice, Mixed Vegetables, Butter[15]

When they were not actively engaged in combat operations, special guard duty, or sentry duty, the routine work of a Marine on board one of the steamers in the Mortar Flotilla was not terribly exciting or difficult. As Private Riddell described the Marine's daily duty schedule on board *Clifton*, it typically meant standing guard for two hours, then having six hours off, followed by a shift of two hours on and eight hours off. *Clifton's* Marine Guard consisted of twelve privates, two corporals, and one sergeant. This made for crowded and uncomfortable conditions below deck in the small space assigned to house the Marines. Riddell complained to his mother that "our berth deck is only 2 feet 6 inches high and we are bent [over] all the time when we are below [deck]."[16]

Gusley candidly admits that the life of a marine was frequently "monotonous," noting that on many occasions "events of any note are of so rare occurrence that it is almost useless to waste paper on a Note-Book to record them." Nevertheless, even during these periods of inactivity, Gusley's Note-Book offers a unique glimpse into the daily routine on board a Navy warship. Noting that "the life of a marine is a diversification of numerous tedious, useful, and even scientific occupations," he records in the Note-Book activities ranging from coal-heaving to picket duty.[17]

One thing that strikes many readers of Gusley's Note-Book is how frequently and abruptly his ships change position. Gusley literally does not know when he lies down to sleep where the next day will find him. On one occasion in the summer of 1862, he laments that "transitory, indeed, is our present life," observing that "each succeeding twenty-four hours finds us at a different place."[18] Gusley's journeys take him from New York to New Orleans and from Florida to Texas, with long voyages up the Mississippi River and through the swamps of Louisiana in between. In recording his impressions of these widely scattered places, Gusley's Note-Book offers valuable descriptions of many ports and towns throughout the South.

## About the Mortar Flotilla

When the Civil War erupted, Union military planners lost no time in spreading out their maps of the Confederacy to devise a strategy for capturing and holding the rebellion's most important places. A single city—New Orleans—emerged at the top of nearly every strategist's list of targets and objectives. The South's largest city and busiest port, New Orleans was located a little more than one hundred miles above the mouth of the Mississippi River, thus controlling passage on America's greatest artery of commerce. Until New Orleans was safely in Union hands, it was clear that Northern trade was in jeopardy and the rebellious South could never be truly deemed to have been subdued.

Although it was evident to officials planning the Union war effort that New Orleans needed to be occupied as soon as possible, such a conquest did not at first seem easily achievable. Forts Jackson and St. Philip, a pair of massive brick fortifications joined by a chain, flanked the Mississippi River below that city. Designed before the war to be among America's most powerful fortifications, these forts appeared to be so strong to military planners on both sides of the conflict that it had become almost an article of faith that they could not be overcome by naval forces moving up the river. Instead, military strategists on both sides assumed, it would be necessary for the Union Navy to move south along the entire course of the Mississippi, capturing New Orleans only at the end of a prolonged campaign that would involve occupying and capturing every important Confederate city (including the citadel at Vicksburg) upriver from New Orleans.

How did it come to pass that New Orleans eventually became one of the first (instead of the last) large cities in the South to be captured by the Union? The answer revolves around a duel between "ship and shore" that would play its way out throughout the duration of the Civil War. It was a duel that Nestell and Gusley would witness firsthand.

Not long after the beginning of the war, the United States Navy experienced some remarkable success along the Atlantic coast in overcoming Confederate forts.[19] This early success (soon reinforced by the capture of some key forts on western rivers) led to an important change of strategy. The Navy's successes in capturing Confederate forts encouraged Union war department officials to begin asking themselves a question that had formerly been viewed as almost unthinkable: Could the same naval power that had produced victories over Confederate forts on the east coast and western rivers now be used to directly challenge and overcome the powerful forts flanking the Mississippi River below New Orleans? For such a scheme to have any chance of success, two big problems would have to be solved. First, the swampy conditions prevailing below New Orleans made it virtually impossible to capture the forts using armies and conventional land siege tactics. Surveys confirmed that the dismal, wet terrain made it physically impractical to move heavy artillery pieces into positions from which a force of infantry and artillery could effectively attack the Confederate forts. If the forts were to be attacked, that attack would have to come almost exclusively from the water.

The necessity of a naval attack compounded the second problem that the Union military faced on the lower Mississippi: any naval force powerful enough to face and overcome the pounding it was bound to suffer from the Confederate guns known to be mounted in the forts below New Orleans would, of necessity, include a large number of big warships; such vessels, however, were by nature heavy and deep in draft and would encounter great difficulty passing over the sandbars deposited outside the fanlike entrances to the Mississippi River. Each of these problems (launching an artillery attack from the river and getting the large warships involved in that attack into the river) would have to be overcome if an attack on New Orleans up the Mississippi River was going to be seriously considered.

After giving the matter some careful thought, Commander David Dixon Porter came up with a proposed solution for the problem of how to launch a bombardment from the river.[20] His plan for capturing these forts, based on his experience blockading the mouth of the Mississippi River, involved conducting a lengthy and continuous bombardment using a large number of heavy mortars. To move these heavy mortars into firing distance of the Confederate forts despite the swampy terrain, Porter proposed the creation of a "Mortar Flotilla" that would consist of a fleet of specially designed schooners equipped with immense mortars mounted securely on their reinforced decks. These "bombers," or "mortar boats," as they were also called, were intended to serve collectively as a floating battery. The Confederates would later derisively refer to these mortar vessels as "spit boxes," but to Union war planners they seemed to be the key to unlocking the gates to the Mississippi River. Realizing the critical importance of seizing New Orleans at an early date, as well as the absence of any good alternatives, the U.S. Navy finally adopted Porter's plan. On February 10, 1862, the Mortar Flotilla (initially called the "Bomb Flotilla") was formally created to serve under Commander Porter's orders.[21]

The motto of the Mortar Flotilla might well have been "Have mortar—will travel." Twenty schooners that had originally been purchased for use as light cruisers were quickly fitted out with one thirteen-inch mortar each (Figure 3). They also carried from two to four other guns along their sides. The "chowderheads," as the large mortars were affectionately referred to by the men hastily assembled to operate them, were about four feet wide at the muzzle and five feet in length. Each mortar weighed about 18,000 pounds and was mounted on an iron carriage (Figure 4) that weighed about 10,000 pounds. Placed on a revolving table or bed (Figure 5), the whole

FIGURE 3. The Deck of a Mortar Schooner in Porter's Mortar Fleet. Courtesy of U.S. Army Military History Institute, Carlisle, Pennsylvania.

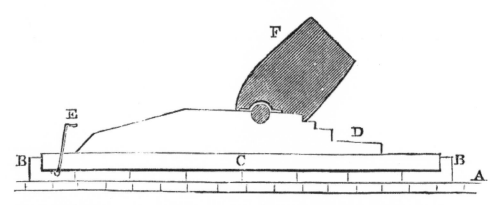

FIGURE 4. Diagram of a 13-inch Mortar Mounted on a Mortar Boat Showing (A) the Deck, (B) the Stationary Bed, (C) the Circle, (D) the Mortar Slide, (E) the Crank, and (F) the Mortar. From *Harper's Weekly*.

mortar assembly weighed between 16 and 17 tons. When completed, the mortar schooners varied in size between 160 to 200 tons and carried a crew of about forty men each.[22]

Operating as a coordinated squadron, these mortar vessels were capable of delivering a massive quantity of shell and shot raining down on any target that might be designated. Commander Porter's plan required that these vessels be designed to withstand the punishment resulting from delivering heavy bombardments continuously for a period that might extend day and night for weeks. The specially reinforced mortars were cast in Pittsburgh and transported to New York and Philadelphia along with 30,000 bombshells. The mortar carriages were made in New York.[23]

To withstand the massive stress that such a bombardment would necessarily inflict on the vessels that delivered it, the mortar schooners were filled in almost solidly beneath their decks with a complex web of timber supports (Figure 6). These supports were intended to function basically as shock absorbers when the mortar was fired. The shells to be fired from the mortars each weighed 216 pounds, contained 11 pounds of powder, and when fired with the usual

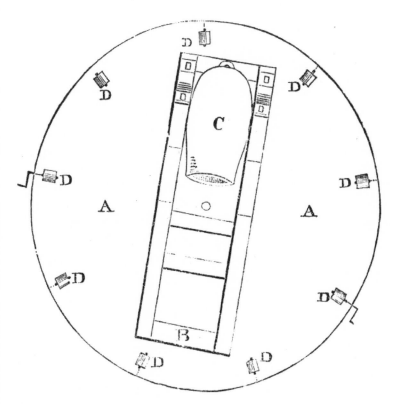

FIGURE 5. Diagram of the Circular Mounting of a 13-inch Mortar on a Mortar Boat Showing (A) Mortar Bed, (B) Slide, (C) Mortar, and (D) Rollers. From *Harper's Weekly*.

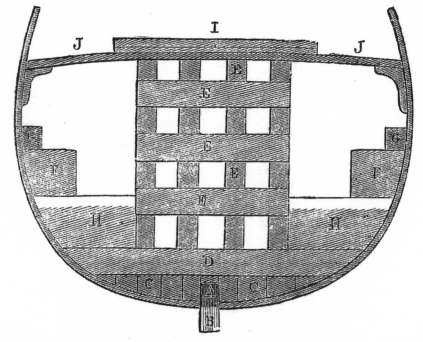

A, Keelson.—B, Keel.—C, Oak filling.—D, Oak floor timbers.—E. Pine cross-timbers.—F, Lockers.—G, Hummock lockers.—H, Water tanks.—I, Mortar bed.—J, Main deck.

FIGURE 6. Cross section of a Mortar Boat Showing Reinforced Mortar Bed. From *Harper's Weekly*.

20-pound service charge of powder had an expected range of 4,200 yards.[24]

The men assigned to the Mortar Flotilla were for the most part not experienced naval personnel. Like Henry Gusley and Dr. Nestell, they were ordinary men who had volunteered to serve in their country's naval forces. Some of the crewmen had served in the merchant marine. But many of the men, particularly those assigned to actually service the mortars, had no experience with the sea whatsoever. For example, an Irishman named Pat joined Porter's mortar expedition after serving three months in the Army. Pat had been convinced by his friends that service in the Navy simply had to be better than the harsh military life he was experiencing with the U.S. Army on land. Based on this reasoning, he volunteered for the Navy as soon as his three-month Army enlistment expired. Because he had no nautical experience of any kind, however, Pat was immediately assigned the worst duties on the ship, which included the miserable job of serving as lookout during bad weather. One night during a particularly violent storm the men below deck could hear Pat at his post on deck cursing and swearing in a loud voice: "O holy Moses! The divil take me fri'nds sure! Ah! me fri'nds advised me to go to sea in the navy, and not go in the army ag'in, for a sailor, says they, always has a house over his head; but the very divil was in them when they gave me that advice sure!"[25]

Going to sea was not the only bad advice that men like Pat received. As it turned out, they received inadequate and occasionally erroneous instruction in how to safely operate the guns on their vessels. Firing a four-ton mortar was a complicated and frequently dangerous procedure, as Theodore R. Davis, special artist for *Harper's Weekly*, explained:

> The mortar, by means of a mathematical instrument, is pointed at the exact elevation of 45 degrees. A wooden bar, or sight, with a spirit-level attached, is then firmly screwed to the trunnion, and the exact position of the mortar at its elevation of 45 degrees is marked upon it. With the distance to be fired varies the charge of powder, each charge being carefully weighed and placed in the mortar loose, instead of in cartridge. When the distance fired is very great, and the charge of powder in consequence large, the men—to avoid the effect of the heavy concussion—stand on tip-toe and with mouths open. The open mouth allows the sound to reach the inside of the ear-drum, reduces the effect of the concussion, and renders the shock much less severe.[26]

The advice given to mortar crews to open their mouths and stand on tiptoes was good as far as it went, but, in truth, a flotilla of mortar vessels did not fit the usual navy procedures very well, and there was little experience to guide the men who were expected to actually operate the huge guns on these vessels. Most of the mortar crews arrived in the Gulf of Mexico without having fired the mortars on their ships even a single time. As one naval officer described the situation, when the mortar crews finally got the opportunity to test their principal weapons (Figure 7), there were some real surprises:

> We went through all the preparations for action; loaded the mortar with a full-service charge of twenty pounds of powder, cut a fuse for four thousand yards, and, after several changes of sighting from one side and then the other, I gave the order to fire. The crew, according to the manual, had been taught to "stand in the rear of the piece on tip-toe, with mouth and ears open;" but, as this was

FIGURE 7. Firing from a Mortar Schooner. From *Harper's Weekly*.

real, and I did not know just what the thing would do, I
ordered them farther away, while I, with my officers, noted
the time of flight of the shell, and the time of sound from
the explosion of the shell; after which I took a survey of
the deck. The mortar had recoiled off the turntable back
against the side, driving the rear of the carriage into the
water-ways, and listing the vessel about ten degrees. The
concussion had taken nearly every door off the hinges,
the arms-chest and round-houses collapsed, and other
slight damage. [The previously mentioned Irish crewman]
Pat was the first to call attention. He stood fixed with his
hands upon his hips, looking at the mortar-carriage stuck
in the water-way. "O howly Jasus, and wouldant I have
been in the hell of a fix, if I had stayed where they tould
me? Sure me legs would have been gone entirely!" Such
really would have been the case. For my discovery I was
rewarded with a "day off" and breechings were ordered
to be fitted on the mortars of all the vessels.[27]

Because the mortar schooners carried a wide variety and sizes of
powder charges and ammunition in addition to their heavy mortars,

these vessels necessarily tended to be heavy ships. A steam engine would have made such a ship even heavier, making it difficult for the mortar vessel to enter the Mississippi River and reach its station within firing range of the Confederate forts. In addition, the presence of so much powder and ammunition on the schooners made it dangerous to have on board the type of flame that would have been associated with the typical steam engines of the day. This meant that the mortar schooners would have to be powered by sail, to the extent that they had any power of independent movement at all. As a practical matter, it became obvious that in most cases the mortar schooners would actually need to be towed into position by steamers equipped for that purpose. This brought up and in fact compounded the second problem that needed to be solved in Commander Porter's plan to capture New Orleans: getting big ships over the sandbars at the entrance to the Mississippi River. As the mortar schooners neared completion, Porter could clearly see that he needed steamers not only to get the large gunboats into the river but also to tow his own flotilla of mortars up the river and into position to support the attack on the Confederate forts.

Porter satisfied his need for steamers by creating a "steamer division" in his flotilla. To head this division, two large ferryboats were acquired and converted into gunboats. It was on these two steamers that Henry Gusley and Dr. Daniel Nestell would eventually serve. The first ship acquired for the steamer division, the steamer on which Gusley left New York for the South, was U.S.S. *Westfield* (Figure 8), which was a side-wheel steamer of 822 tons that had been purchased from Cornelius Vanderbilt for $90,000 in November 1861. Prior to its purchase, *Westfield* had been in use as a Staten Island ferryboat. Equipped as a gunboat, *Westfield* mounted six guns, the largest of which was a 100-pounder Parrott rifle.[28]

The other steamer—another converted ferryboat—was U.S.S. *Clifton* (named for Clifton, New Jersey). Purchased by the U.S. Navy, likewise for $90,000, in December 1861 from the New York Union Ferry Company, *Clifton* (Figure 9) was a side-wheel steamer of 892 tons. At 210 feet long it was 5 feet shorter than *Westfield*, but at 40 feet its beam was 5 feet wider. *Clifton* usually mounted eight guns, including a 30-pounder Parrott rifle.[29]

Ferryboats (Figure 10) like *Clifton* and *Westfield* had never been intended by their builders to travel vast distances on the open ocean, and there were substantial doubts in the Navy that they would even be able to reach their stations far to the south in the Gulf of Mexico. Those fears seemed well founded when the ferryboats were

FIGURE 8. U.S.S. *Westfield*. From ORN, vol. 19.

FIGURE 9. The *Clifton* Butting a Fire Raft. Sketch No. 15 by Dr. Daniel D. T. Nestell. Courtesy of the Nimitz Library, U.S. Naval Academy, Annapolis, Maryland.

battered by substantial Atlantic storms and suffered significant damage almost as soon as they left New York waters. One pessimistic Marine on board *Clifton* wrote home to his family as they made the long journey south to Key West that "all hands expect to go to the bottom."[30] Eventually, the Mortar Flotilla reached the Gulf of Mexico, where the fighting ferryboats would prove their critics wrong. As one naval writer has characterized this movement, "Off they gamely waddled. Like the bee, which is held aerodynamically incapable of flight yet flies anyhow, the ferryboats did not understand that they could not go into the open ocean, and they steamed obliviously forth."[31]

When the Mortar Flotilla finally joined the Union armada at the mouth of the Mississippi, Commodore David Glasgow Farragut was not exactly delighted to see it.[32] Farragut's orders provided that "when these formidable mortars arrive, and you are completely ready, you will collect such vessels as can be spared from the blockade, and proceed up the Mississippi River, and reduce the defenses which guard the approaches to New Orleans."[33] But Farragut had never been very comfortable with this part of the plan. In fact, when the Mortar Flotilla's part in the plan of attack had first been revealed to him in Washington, Farragut politely but dismissively commented

FIGURE 10. Slightly Smaller Than *Westfield* and *Clifton*, the Ferryboat U.S.S. *Commodore Perry* Was Converted into a Gunboat Carrying Two 9-inch and Two 32-Pounder Guns as Well as a 100-Pounder Rifle. National Archives and Records Administration.

that "he placed little reliance on mortars, and that they would not have been part of his plan and advisement, but that he would take the mortar-fleet with him, as it had been adopted as part of the equipment of the fleet and might prove of more advantage than he anticipated."[34]

Although Farragut still retained doubts about the utility of the mortar schooners, the steamer division of the flotilla, particularly *Westfield* and *Clifton*, proved immediately valuable. Within eight hours of their arrival at the mouth of the Mississippi River, the steamers had towed into the river all twenty-one mortar vessels of the Mortar Flotilla and were ready to lend assistance to the rest of the Navy's expedition (Figure 11). This was hard work. The Mississippi at this position contained one sandbar after another, and to compound the problem, the bottoms of the winding channels were littered with sunken vessels, chains, and machinery. While pulling *Pensacola* and *Mississippi* over the bar, both of which had displacement weights of 3,000 tons or more, *Clifton* broke all three of its hawsers (heavy ropes used in towing). One of these breakages caused a fragment of the hawser to whip back, killing one crewman on *Pensacola* and breaking the legs of two others.[35] Despite these setbacks, the ferryboats continued their critical and difficult work. *Westfield* and *Clifton*, in particular, were put to good use hauling some of the largest gunboats ever to enter the Mississippi River over the bar and into the river. Commander Porter reported proudly to Washington that these two steamers quickly proved themselves to be "the two most effective vessels in these waters."[36]

Beginning on the morning of April 18, 1862, the mortar schooners were towed up the Mississippi River (usually in groups of four at a time) and anchored at positions that had been carefully mapped out by representatives of the Coast Survey. At great personal risk to themselves and their survey steamer (*Sachem*), the Coast Survey officers surveyed the precise firing positions of the mortar schooners to determine as closely as possible the perfect places from which to bombard the Confederate forts below New Orleans.

The first day's bombardment saw the firing of almost 1,100 shells from the mortar schooners, many of which appeared to burst within the walls of the forts.[37] As it turned out, this first day of the bombardment was by far the most effective of any day in the siege that followed. Colonel Edward Higgins, the Confederate commander whose headquarters was within Fort Jackson, said that dawn on the second day brought a "terrible scene of destruction" within the fort. Although the fort's guns themselves were

FIGURE 11. U.S.S. *Westfield* (Middle Left) and *Clifton* (Middle Right) Assist Farragut's Fleet to Enter the Mississippi River. From *Harper's Weekly*.

not badly injured, at the end of the bombardment nearly five days later, Higgins admitted "everything else in and around the fort was destroyed."[38]

There was considerable controversy, even during the war, as to how effective Porter's mortar bombardment had actually been. As Colonel Higgins admitted, to the Confederates inside the forts the bombardment had seemed an awesome thing, causing substantial damage to the walls of the forts and the structures within them. Assistant Surveyor Joseph Harris of the U.S. Coast Survey, who conducted a survey of Fort Jackson after it eventually surrendered,

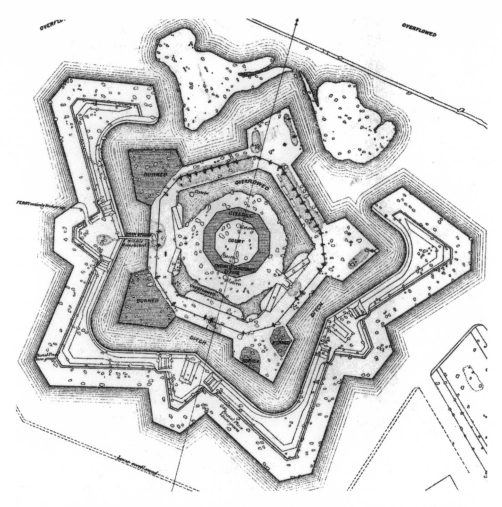

FIGURE 12. U.S. Coast Survey Plan of Fort Jackson. Dark Sections Showing Damage from the Mortar Flotilla's Bombardment, April 18–24, 1862. From ORN, vol. 18.

observed that "the ramparts of the fort proper were severely damaged on every side, but particularly on the two northern ones" (Figure 12). Noting that every building in the fort had been destroyed either by fire or bombshell and that the walls, casemates, and bastions were so cracked that he could see daylight through some of them, Harris concluded that "the impression left on my mind is of a place far gone on the road to ruin, which will stand but little more before it will come down about its defenders' ears."[39]

Other naval officers, particularly those close to Flag Officer Farragut, took a different view of the effectiveness of the mortar bombardment. Conceding that considerable damage had been done to the buildings within the forts and that the walls had indeed been cracked in some places, Porter's critics observed that the main strategic targets of this bombardment—the guns facing the river—had suffered relatively little damage during the bombardment. Instead, the critics pointed out, every time the Union fleet approached the forts, even after ninety-six hours of supposedly heavy bombardment, the defensive fire from the forts seemed as vigorous as ever. As a consequence of this failure to damage the key element of the enemy's war-making power (his guns), Farragut apparently lost the little faith he had ever had in mortars and determined to adopt a risky strategy of running by the forts at night.[40]

There remains considerable debate even today about the true contribution of Porter's mortar bombardment to the almost miraculous success of Farragut's passage of the forts below New Orleans. The only thing that can be said with any certainty is that the sustained bombardment by Porter's Mortar Flotilla clearly served to wear down the enemy's resistance within the forts to the point that when Farragut's fleet steamed by early on the morning of April 24, 1862, the Confederate forts were unable to concentrate their fire in such a fashion that it would do substantial damage to the Union fleet as it passed. Instead, Farragut's ships steamed past largely unhindered, suffering relatively few casualties and leaving his vessels in such excellent shape that they were able to fight their way through the Confederate fleet (where they suffered the loss of U.S.S. *Varuna* to Confederate rams) and then steam rapidly up to the city of New Orleans the next day and force its surrender. It was a conquest that would send shockwaves throughout the Confederacy.

After assisting Farragut to pass the forts below New Orleans and capture that city, the Mortar Flotilla was next employed in operations against the Confederate citadel at Vicksburg. This operation proved unsuccessful when the Army was unable to move troops into position to successfully support the naval attack and assault Vicksburg. Therefore, with no immediate project in sight, the Mortar Flotilla was withdrawn to the relative safety of Ship Island off the Mississippi coast.

For a while it appeared that Mobile would be the next military target at which the floating mortars would be pointed. But political and economic considerations dictated that Texas was to be the next point of invasion. The steamer division was detached from most of the remainder of the Mortar Flotilla and was sent to Texas on an expedition (ultimately unsuccessful) to capture and hold the important port city of Galveston. During the battle that led to the Confederate recapture of Galveston, U.S.S. *Harriet Lane* (Commander Porter's former flagship) was seized by the rebels, and *Westfield* was destroyed by its Union captain to keep it out of the enemy's hands.

It was at this point that Henry Gusley (who was not on *Westfield* at the time of its destruction) was transferred to serve as part of the Marine Guard on *Clifton*. For the next nine months, *Clifton* and the remaining vessels in the steamer division were used in a series of operations along the Gulf Coast. Some of these operations, like the capture of the Confederate fort at Butte a la Rose in Louisiana, were important victories that helped extend Union control of shallow inland rivers. Still other operations involved routine blockading duty in Mississippi Sound and defensive patrols off of Ship Island.

In September 1863, the Army decided to once again attack Texas, this time choosing to begin the invasion at what was supposed to be a lightly guarded point—Sabine Pass. But on September 8, 1863, the Union invasion was turned back at the pass by fewer than fifty Confederates, leading to the capture of *Clifton* and its crew. This effectively eliminated the steamer division of the Mortar Flotilla as an organized fighting force. Mortars would be used again by the Navy, most notably against large forts on the Atlantic Coast like Fort Fisher. But the Mortar Flotilla that had been sent south with Porter to the Gulf of Mexico had served its purpose, and its remaining elements were divided up and assigned to other duties.

## About the Engravings

In addition to the drawings by Dr. Daniel D. T. Nestell, Gusley's Note-Book is illustrated in this book with engravings and etchings from the period during and immediately following the Civil War. Although photography existed at the time of the war, and famous photos by Matthew Brady and other pioneering photographers provide an important record of a relatively small number of the places and events of that war, photographs were not the primary means of capturing and sharing images to a population eager for news about the progress of the war. To begin with, photographic equipment was bulky and cumbersome to transport, making it particularly difficult for photographers to capture images of active operations like naval campaigns. The technology of the time required steady cameras and relatively long exposures, making it almost impossible to record any battles. Weather conditions also made photography difficult and unreliable. Even if it had been possible to capture battle images on film, it was not possible to reproduce such photos commercially in publications like newspapers in which the public could view them in a timely fashion.

To solve the problem of mass distribution of wartime images,

FIGURE 13. Photograph of David D. Porter and Depiction of the Same Scene in *Harper's Weekly*. Courtesy of the Naval Historical Center.

periodicals like *Frank Leslie's Illustrated Newspaper* and *Harper's Weekly* sent teams, composed of correspondents and talented "special artists" like Winslow Homer, William Waud, and Edwin Forbes, to document battles and military movements throughout the South. Their eyewitness sketches were then shipped north, where they were redrawn on wood and eventually transformed into engravings.[41] Where a photograph existed, the popular publications often raced to scoop their competitors in transforming it into an engraving, which was then quickly and efficiently made the centerpiece of an article that would capture the eye of a prospective reader. In this process, details were frequently omitted or changed in order to make for a more interesting and attractive image. As an example of this transformation, Figure 13 is a side-by-side comparison of a photograph of Commander David Dixon Porter with the engraved version of that same photograph that made its way into the pages of *Harper's Weekly* in January 1865. Although largely faithful to the original, the engraving substituted a couple of strategically posed officers and some busy crewmen for what would otherwise have been a fuzzy and uninteresting background.

Depicting naval scenes was particularly challenging for Civil War artists. To begin with, it was difficult—and sometimes dangerous— to get the type of commanding view that was required to make an accurate image. This is illustrated in Figure 14, a dramatic representation of artist William Waud sketching an engagement near

FIGURE 14. William Waud Sketching the Naval Engagement Between the Federal Fleet and the Confederate Forts, Rams, and Gunboats, on the Mississippi River, from the Foretop of the U.S. War Steamer *Mississippi*. From *The Soldier in Our Civil War*, vol. 1.

the mouth of the Mississippi River from the foretop of a warship. Conditions on board a ship during battle, including smoke, deck movement, and noise, made it hard for any artist to work while a fight was in progress. Therefore, Waud (and even nonprofessional artists like Dr. Daniel D. T. Nestell, who made most of the drawings in this book) often merely made rough sketches during the battle showing the positions of the various ships and forts that were engaged. After the battle, they then filled in the details as circumstances permitted. Some of Dr. Nestell's sketches were never completed, containing only a notation in pencil that a particular ship or building was at a specified location in the scene. Where it will aid the reader's understanding of a particular scene, the editor has added caption boxes to some of Dr. Nestell's drawings. These boxes render more legible and sometimes expand on the notes made by the artist when the sketches were originally made.

## About African Americans and the Navy

Henry Gusley's Note-Book confirms that he was a man of his time insofar as racial relations were concerned. His Note-Book referred to black people by a variety of racial epithets, most of which the editor has changed (with changes noted) to less offensive terms. There is also little about Gusley's views on the institution of slavery that would differentiate him from the Southerners against whom he fought. Noting that the slaves he saw working on shore in the South seemed to have more time off than the crew on his own ship, Gusley pronounced the "much talked of hardships of the Southern slave" to be a myth.[42] Gusley was not alone in his views on race and slavery. As historian Michael J. Bennett has noted, "based on their letters and diaries, the overwhelming majority of Union sailors harbored every vicious, condescending prejudice ruminating in American society concerning blacks in the mid-nineteenth century."[43]

In addition to doubting the merits of emancipation, Gusley also expressed clear reservations about the institution of slavery as an appropriate precipitating cause of the war. He believed extremist agitators on both sides of the slavery issue shared the blame for causing the war, and he was not convinced that the conflict was really necessary. If slavery was the main issue, he insisted, then there was no justification for the war because, as far as he could see, slavery had "no deteriorating effect upon the country." Since Gusley regretted the role that agitation over slavery had played in precipitating the war, he was surprised (as were many Northern sailors) when President Lincoln made it a central focus of the war with the issuance of the Emancipation Proclamation.[44] Disgusted to hear that emancipation had been officially sanctioned, Gusley recorded sarcastically in his Note-Book that when he enlisted he thought that it was for the purpose of preserving the Union. Now, he lamented, it was beginning to look like the real purpose of the war had all along been the abolition of slavery. "Strange," Gusley observed, "how circumstances will alter opinions."[45]

One of the most interesting features in Gusley's Note-Book is the evolution it reflects in its author's perception of emancipation. As Gusley's service extended into the spring of 1863, he continued to have more direct and personal encounters with the emancipated slaves who served on board his ship. The number and tone of the racial epithets in his Note-Book gradually subsided, and Gusley eventually came to favor the Emancipation Proclamation that he had so bitterly opposed when it was issued. Justifying it on the ground that such a policy takes slave labor that would otherwise be useful to the enemy and puts it to use for the Union cause, Gusley insists that "this sounds like abolitionism, but it is not—we call it logic."[46] This "logic," as Gusley terms it, led to an increasing number of black sailors in the U.S. Navy. By some estimates, black men comprised almost 20 percent of the Navy's crews by the end of the war.[47] Gusley's Note-Book is thus a fascinating record of one of the most important developments in the history of America's armed services: the freeing and eventually the training and arming of African Americans.

# Galveston Tri-Weekly News
## *Introduction to the Note-Book*

The following is the commencement of a Yankee Note-Book found on *Clifton*, which was captured the other day at Sabine Pass.[1] The book is of considerable length, containing some 150 written pages, and closing at the time of the capture. We withhold the writer's name [later revealed to be Henry O. Gusley], and have not yet been able to learn whether he is among the killed or captured. He is evidently an accomplished scholar, and his journal is replete with graphic descriptions of interesting incidents. We have concluded to publish the whole of it in regular order, giving more or less in each issue of our paper until it is finished. It will be seen that he commences his journal on the 3rd of May 1862, but it appears that he commenced his service as a Marine on board the *Westfield* some two or three months earlier, and in the next chapter we shall publish, he goes back to the beginning of his service, and gives an account of the taking of Forts Jackson and St. Philip, and the capture of New Orleans, in which he participated on board the *Westfield*.

# Note-Book

# 1 The Battle Below New Orleans

MAY 3, 1862      A book without a preface is a mystery until it has been thoroughly read; no accurate supposition can be formed of its contents, or its aim, without a title. This being a self-evident proposition, and the writer of this being seized with the idea of perpetuating the different scenes through which he, in his transitory life, may pass, and at the same time, thinking that, at some future day, it may be a source of much edification to himself or some of his friends, or even a means of useful information as to data—to refer to—has determined to note down each and every event of importance that may happen around him. The same mystery that envelops the founding of the immortal "Pickwick Club,"[1] also enshrouds, as regards minutiae, the early career of this writer. We fall upon the renowned members of that club in the midst of one of their momentous meetings; and likewise, at the most momentous period of his life, has this writer imitated the example of the above quoted gentlemen, and opened a Note-Book.

This page, then, dispels all the mystery that we have said exists for want of a preface; and a glance at the ending of the first paragraph at once prevents the forming of any supposition by boldly stating the title [Note-Book].

[Gusley begins his narrative on May 3, five days after the surrender of the forts below New Orleans. In the next entry, dated May 4, however, Gusley goes back in time to catch his readers up on the events leading up to the New Orleans campaign and the successful capture of New Orleans.—Ed.]

The momentous period alluded to is five days after the surrender of Forts Jackson and St. Philip,[2] placed by geographers, as well as by human hands, on a large bend of the Mississippi River, about

FIGURE 15. Running of the Forts by Commodore Farragut's Fleet, April 24, 1862. Sketch No. 9 by Dr. Daniel D. T. Nestell. Courtesy of the Nestell Collection, Nimitz Library, U.S. Naval Academy, Annapolis, Maryland.

FIGURE 16. The U.S. Steamer *Harriet Lane*. Detail from Sketch No. 27 by Dr. Daniel D. T. Nestell. Courtesy of the Nestell Collection, Nimitz Library, U.S. Naval Academy, Annapolis, Maryland.

thirty miles from the mouth of said river and eighty-five from New Orleans. The bombardment was a terrible one, commencing early on Good Friday morning and continuing, day and night, until early on the following Thursday morning, when one division of our fleet was pushed above the forts, after a terrific battle of nearly an hour (Figure 15). The fight, in reality, was commenced on the previous Sunday, our vessel, the *Westfield*,[3] having on that day gone up and engaged two of the rebel steamers, and in conjunction with the *Harriet Lane* (Figure 16),[4] firing at and receiving a brisk return from the forts; and the forts did not surrender until the Monday after the main battle.

———— ➤◦◄ ————

MAY 4, 1862   We belayed our writing yesterday, for the very good reason that it was our turn for two hours' "sentry-go" on the hurricane;[5] and having various other little duties to attend to, after performing that arduous but highly necessary task, we were unable to again add a few more words under the date of the first page. In order to keep up a true record of events according to our first intention, and to carry out the thread of our narrative prior to the date of our conceiving the idea of keeping a Note-Book, we find it necessary to adopt the rule carried out in the manly game of ten-pins when the play becomes a tie, and play it "old and new."[6] We had intended to state (and will do so now) that we were on that date in receipt of a letter from our brother,[7] dated Fort Hyman, Kentucky,[8] March 27th, 1862, which we hastened to answer. In it he stated that his regiment (52nd Indiana) has borne a conspicuous part in the taking of Fort Donelson,[9] and that he was slightly wounded in that engagement. We will also note that on the 1st inst. we received a letter from home, the first since leaving Washington, and which we also answered promptly. Also that we were lying at Pilot Town[10] while writing, and that the said town was situated on the Mississippi River, just below the head of the South-West Pass of that river, and was of no particular note, except being the home of the numerous pilots who are necessary to navigators of the mouths of the "Father of Waters." Before the bombardment of the forts, it was the rendezvous of the war vessels, composing the two fleets, engaged in that undertaking; and even yet it presents quite the appearance of a large seaport town.[11] Today, notwithstanding its being noted in the calendar as Sunday, we are engaged, about ten miles above the said town, in endeavoring to drag a schooner (Figure 17), belonging to the

FIGURE 17. A Mortar Schooner. Sketch No. 80 by Dr. Daniel D. T. Nestell. Courtesy of the Nestell Collection, Nimitz Library, U.S. Naval Academy, Annapolis, Maryland.

fleet, out of a deep and swift sluice into which she drifted during the past week. It has every appearance of proving a long job; but short or long, it is a very disagreeable one, for the surrounding shores are all swamp, and the mosquitoes and sand-flies torment us half to death.[12] People who have never been in this vicinity have no true idea of mosquitoes. A few small ones may be occasionally met with North, but here you can scarcely breathe for them and the other noiseless little insect [sand-flies] before mentioned. It is quite amusing to watch the different persons scattered around the decks, first striking themselves on one spot and then on another, and scratching here and there with a vigor that would make one suppose they all needed a good overhauling with soap and water, did we not know the cause. Here you see one scratching the back of his ear, in strict imitation of an author chasing up some brilliant idea; there another rubbing his hands, for all the world like a Methodist parson at his devotions; and there another striking wildly at some unseen object like one demented. And, besides this, we have the assurance that they are not near so numerous now as they will be a month hence, and also that it is highly probable that we will remain here until that period. How the people along this shore manage to live for them I cannot imagine; but they do not appear to be afraid of them. One of our Yankee soldiers, in strolling by one of the houses on the shore (Figure 18) the other evening, where an old man was sitting smoking his pipe and killing the insects by the hundreds as they lit upon him, remarked by way of starting a conversation with him: "Mosquitoes are pretty troublesome 'round here." "Yaas, said the Southerner, "but they're nothin' to what they used to was," at the same time brushing away like fury. "Do tell!" exclaimed the astonished Yankee, "darned if I kin see room for *many* more," at the same time knocking a huge one (fully as large as a piece of chalk) with such force as to capsize the old man's pipe. "Yaas, I'll stick to it, stranger, but when I come to think uv it, they're summit bigger nor they war."

[At this point, Gusley takes a respite from recording current events and narrates his adventures from February 22, 1862, when he left New York, through his arrival in the Gulf of Mexico and the capture of New Orleans.—Ed.]

But we must again go back to the *Westfield*, which we had left just as she had started from Staten Island.[13] We had a pleasant evening passing down the Narrows,[14] and when we entered upon the broad Atlantic, so calm was it that saving the long, even rolling of our vessel,

FIGURE 18. Pilot Town. From Edward King, *The Great South*.

we scarcely knew, until the morning dawned and showed us nothing but a waste of waters, that we had left the quiet bay (Figure 19).

It was a beautiful Sabbath, our first day at sea. Our swift vessel had, during the last twelve hours, taken us a considerable distance from the extremely cold port in which we lay, and the genial warmth of a Southern sun was already realized by us. We had on a former occasion taken a short trip upon the Atlantic, and the strange rolling of the sea, even when the air is calm, was not novel to us, nor did it cause that strange feeling, known as seasickness, which is experienced by almost every person on first entering the ocean. The day, as I have said, was a beautiful one. The waters were unruffled and rolled in gentle swells, giving our vessel a uniform, rocking motion, as she was propelled swiftly onward. The air was calm and serene, and the sun shone with a comfortable degree of warmth upon us. Sunday, at all times, has a peculiar charm about it. The rich and the poor alike hail it as a day of rest. The devout find time to attend their churches, and join with each other in the worship of their God. The lover of nature, and the poor who are imprisoned in the work-shop all the week, can on this day go forth from the crowded city and breathe the pure air of heaven; they can see and feel the goodness of their Maker in the budding tree, the springing grass, or the beautiful flowers, and feel thankful for the benefits of such a day, and be contented

FIGURE 19. The Sailing of Porter's Mortar Flotilla Showing the Flagship *Octorara* on the Right and the Steamer *Westfield* in the Distance on the Left. From *Harper's Weekly*.

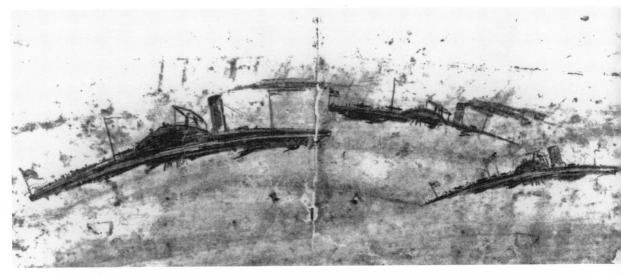

FIGURE 20. The U.S. Steamers *Clifton*, *Westfield*, and *Jackson* in a Storm—February 1862. Sketch No. 1 by Dr. Daniel D. T. Nestell. Courtesy of the Nestell Collection, Nimitz Library, U.S. Naval Academy, Annapolis, Maryland.

and happy. But at sea, with nothing but a waste of waters around us, speckled here and there, perhaps, with a sail, with all unnecessary work belayed, with the awnings spread, and the crew all dressed tidily in clean clothes, one has a deeper feeling of the beauty and solemnity of the day.[15] Even a soldier is not exempt from this feeling, and the writer experienced the same sublime feeling beneath his uniform on this day as he always did when clothed in the garb of a citizen.

The sun went down in the same serenity with which it had risen, but when the moon arose a slight breeze sprung up, which freshened throughout the night, and the next morning found us off the capes of the Virginia Coast, with a stiff gale blowing. Towards night the gale greatly increased, and with such fury did the wind toss the waves that, fearful of being wrecked upon the shore, we stood farther out to sea. The storm (Figure 20) raged with fearful violence during the whole night, and with such force was our vessel pitched about that it was impossible to stand erect, or walk upon the decks; and the sea washed over us to such an extent that the hatches were battened down, leaving us no place to sleep, even if we had the desire to do so.

As the morning dawned, however, the storm abated, and daylight found us over a hundred miles from land, and none of the vessels which started with us in sight. We stood in for the shore, hoping to fall in with our consorts, but not finding them, we stood on our Southerly course, and on Wednesday, the 26th of February, we were

FIGURE 21. The U.S. Steamer *Clifton* off Cape Hatteras—1862. Sketch No. 2 by Dr. Daniel D. T. Nestell. Courtesy of the Nestell Collection, Nimitz Library, U.S. Naval Academy, Annapolis, Maryland.

FIGURE 22. The Beach at Port Royal, South Carolina. From *Harper's Weekly*.

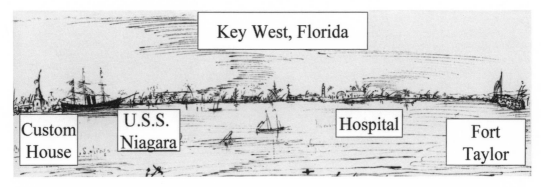

FIGURE 23. View of Key West from *Clifton's* Position. Sketch No. 71 by Dr. Daniel D. T. Nestell. Identification Boxes Added by Editor Replace Same Text Handwritten by Nestell. Courtesy of the Nestell Collection, Nimitz Library, U.S. Naval Academy, Annapolis, Maryland.

off Cape Hatteras, N.C. (Figure 21). In doubling this point of land[16] we experienced a much more terrible storm than the previous one, and we all thought that we should never see the morning's sun.

Some of our planks were torn off by the force of the waves, and about midnight it was discovered that the vessel was making water rapidly. We, however, manned the pumps, and at daylight found ourselves still afloat and the pumps rapidly gaining on the water. That evening we made Port Royal, S.C.,[17] where we remained until the 8th of March for repairs and coal. Port Royal is quite a beautiful little town, and has a very large and commodious harbor. Some time before this it had been captured by the U.S. troops, and was then a place of rendezvous for part of the blockading squadron. An immense navy was riding at anchor in the harbor, and the beach (Figure 22) was lined with the tents of the soldiery. (We wrote a letter home from here on the 1st of March.)

On the 8th, we again put to sea, and on the 10th we arrived at Key West, Florida,[18] having exceedingly fine weather during the trip. Key West is a fine little island at the entrance to the Gulf of Mexico. There is a smart little town (Figure 23) with a fine, deep harbor on the island and a large fort and barracks belonging to the United States. The fort is called Fort Taylor (Figure 24)[19] and is one of the largest belonging to the Government. It mounts over 200 guns. Spring was reigning here in all its beauty, and oranges and bananas freshly plucked from the trees were quite a luxury to us, who, little more than a fortnight before were among ice and snow. We were here rejoined by one of our consorts, the *Clifton*, and the squadron which we were to join having gone to Ship Island, we, on the 13th, weighed anchor and followed them. On the 15th we made Apala-

FIGURE 24. Fort Taylor Near Key West, Florida. From *Frank Leslie's Illustrated Famous Leaders and Battle Scenes of the Civil War.*

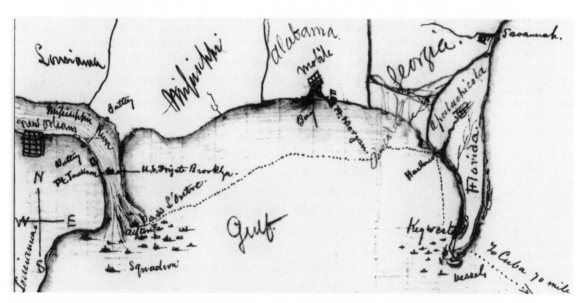

FIGURE 25. Route (Dotted Line) from Key West to the Pass a l'Outre, Showing Fleet at the Entrance to the Mississippi River and the Forts Below New Orleans. Sketch No. 4 by Dr. Daniel D. T. Nestell. Courtesy of the Nestell Collection, Nimitz Library, U.S. Naval Academy, Annapolis, Maryland.

FIGURE 26. Frigates *Pensacola* and *Mississippi* (Center) Aground at Southwest Pass of Mississippi River with *Clifton* (Bottom), *Harriet Lane* (Lower Left), and *Westfield* (Top Left) Engaged Towing Them Off. Sketch No. 3 by Dr. Daniel D. T. Nestell. Courtesy of the Nestell Collection, Nimitz Library, U.S. Naval Academy, Annapolis, Maryland.

chicola, where we remained until the 17th, when we proceeded to the mouth of the Mississippi river, reaching Passe a l'Outre (Figure 25)[20] the next day, and were engaged at this point for the following two weeks in towing the sailing vessels of the fleet over the bar and tugging off those of the larger vessels (Figure 26) which had run aground.[21]

While here we learned that the *R. B. Forbes*[22] had been lost in the storm off [Cape] Hatteras, and the [*John P.*] *Jackson*[23] was compelled to put back to Baltimore for repairs.

———◦◦———

MAY 6, 1862 The life of a marine is a diversification of numerous tedious, useful, and even scientific occupations. He is his own washerwoman; he must be an adept with the needle, in order to keep his clothes in a tidy condition; he is a burnisher of fine brass and a polisher of steel diurnally, in order that his accoutrements may pass inspection; one day (or rather one hour) he is a soldier—the next a sailor; and when the ship is going through the process of coaling, he may be found upon the coal whip[24] and be denominated a coal-heaver (Figure 27). When at sea, and when the morning's work is finished up, he finds plenty of leisure to devote to such occupations or pastimes as his inclinations may lead to, and which is spent in many various ways, such as reading, writing diaries (?) or carving useful ornamental articles with his knife—the

FIGURE 27. Coal Heavers of U.S.S. *Essex*—Resting. G. H. Suydam Collection, Mss. 1394, Louisiana and Lower Mississippi Valley Collections, LSU Libraries, Louisiana State University, Baton Rouge, Louisiana.

latter of which may be called the *scientific* part we have intimated. It is said that from long-continued service in this corps, some of the members of it have become encrusted with a covering like a turtle. It is known, at least to the writer, that we are usually denominated by land soldiers and sailors "shell-backs," and also that we become so addicted to the use of beans, salt pork and salt beef (which latter is metaphorically styled *salt horse*), that any deviation from that food attempted to be forced upon them would be met with the same threat as the Irishman's when they commenced feeding him with cod-fish. "Pork and beans," said he, "as much as you please; but be jabers if you come with any more of your salt cod I'll lave the house." But to return to our narrative.

After getting all the vessels safely over the bar [at the South West Pass entrance to the Mississippi River], we all proceeded up the river to Pilot Town, (before mentioned,) which was to be the place of rendezvous of the fleets to be engaged in the capture of New Orleans. The following is a list of the vessels[25] composing the fleets: They were commanded by Commodores Farragut and Porter. Frigates—*Colorado* and *Mississippi*; Sloops-of-War—*Hartford, Brooklyn, Pensacola, Richmond* (steamers), *Vandalia* and *Portsmouth* (sailers); Gunboats—*Harriet Lane, Westfield, Clifton, Oneida, Owasco, Verona* [*Varuna*], *Miami, Iroquois, Sciota, Kennebec, Wissahickon, Ithasea* [*Itasca*], *Pinola, Cayuga, Wynona* [*Winona*], *Sachem, Jackson,* and *Kinon* [*Kineo*]; and twenty-one [mortar] schooners, each carrying two broadside thirty-twos [32-pounders] and a thirteen-inch mortar—making in all forty-seven vessels, and mounting an average of 440 guns of large caliber.

We were busily engaged until Sunday, the 13th of April, painting our vessels with Mississippi mud—not for the purpose of ornamenting them, but that they might be less conspicuous to the gunners at the [Confederate] forts—and in covering the top masts of the bomb schooners with limbs of trees (Figure 28), in order to make them less liable to be distinguished from the dense wood which lined the river bank near the forts. On this day the *Westfield, Harriet Lane, Clifton,* and *Owasco* made a reconnaissance of the forts, and exchanged a few shots with them and with the two rebel steamers—the *Westfield* being in the advance (Figure 29) and opening the fire.[26] We have since learned that one of our rifle

FIGURE 28. The Masquerade of War—Ingenious Method of Disguising the Masts and Hulls of Commodore Porter's Mortar Flotilla With Boughs of Trees, etc. to Deceive the Confederate Artillerists. From *Frank Leslie's Illustrated Famous Leaders and Battle Scenes of the Civil War.*

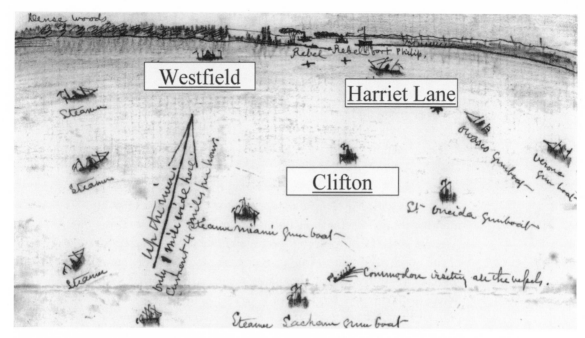

FIGURE 29. The Steamer Division of the Mortar Flotilla Engaging the Forts (Top Center) Below New Orleans. Sketch No. 5 by Dr. Daniel D. T. Nestell. Identification Boxes Added by Editor, Replace Same Text Handwritten by Nestell. Courtesy of the Nestell Collection, Nimitz Library, U.S. Naval Academy, Annapolis, Maryland.

FIGURE 30. *Westfield* (Lower Left) and *Clifton* (Lower Center) at the Bombardment of the Forts below New Orleans by the Mortar Schooners (Numbered on Each Side of the Mississippi River). Title Box Added by Editor Replaces Same Text Handwritten by Nestell. Sketch No. 7 Drawn by Dr. Daniel D. T. Nestell. Courtesy of the Nestell Collection, Nimitz Library, U.S. Naval Academy, Annapolis, Maryland.

FIGURE 31. U.S.S. *Westfield* Protects Fleet from Enemy Fire Rafts Below New Orleans. From *The Soldier in Our Civil War*, vol. 1.

shots sunk one of the rebel steamers.[27] No one was hurt on our side, although the enemy's shot fell in close proximity to us.

On Friday, the 18th, having got the fleet into position, we commenced bombarding (Figure 30) and continued our fire day and night until the following Thursday morning, the 24th, when after a terrific battle of nearly an hour (Figure 31), we succeeded in getting our heavy vessels above the forts, with but comparatively small loss.

A bombardment (Figure 32) is a terrible scene, but at the same time one not altogether devoid of grandeur and sublimity.[28] After the first few shots, the screaming of the huge shell and the whistling of the shot lose their terrific sounds, and a complete callousness to all danger appears to take possession of all. One becomes used to the blinding flash of the powder and the deafening roar of the artillery, and the sulphurous smell at first so stifling appears to impart to the atmosphere an invigorating tendency. The fiery tracks of the bombs at night are traced with feelings of the most intense interest in those who have sent them forth on their mission of death; and as their rushing noise gradually becomes less distinct, and they hang like a bright star for a moment over the fort, and then explode with a deep roar, scattering destruction, perhaps death, within its walls, a shout of triumph is heard from the ships, mingling in strange contrast with the din of the battle. Everything is forgotten, save to destroy, and when at night some continue the strife and others are detailed to bury those who have been killed during the day, they hurry to

FIGURE 32. The Fleet Engaging the Two Forts—3:30 A.M., April 24, 1862, "From a Chance Sketch As I Could." Sketch No. 8 by Dr. Daniel D. T. Nestell. Courtesy of the Nestell Collection, Nimitz Library, U.S. Naval Academy, Annapolis, Maryland.

FIGURE 33. Commander Porter Receiving Confederate Officers on the *Harriet Lane*. From *Battles and Leaders*, vol. 2.

FIGURE 34. General Butler's Troops Passing Through a Bayou in the Rear of Fort St. Philip. Sketch No. 16 by Dr. Daniel D. T. Nestell. Courtesy of the Nestell Collection, Nimitz Library, U.S. Naval Academy, Annapolis, Maryland.

the beach and place them under the sod with as much dispatch as possible. Graphically, indeed, has the burial of the heroes of Fort Jackson[29] been described in the burial of the hero of Corruna:[30]

> We buried them darkly, in dead of night,
> The turf with our bayonets turning,
> By the struggling moonbeam's misty light,
> And our lanterns dimly burning.
> Few and short were the prayers we said,
> And we breathed but a word of sorrow,
> But we steadfastly gazed on the face of the dead,
> And bitterly thought on the morrow.
> No useless coffins confined their breasts,
> Nor in sheets nor in shrouds we bound them.
> But they lay like warriors taking their rest
> With their martial cloaks around them.

The fleet below the forts (to which the *Westfield* was attached) kept up their firing until Sunday, the 27th, when a flag of truce was sent to us, asking [for] a cessation of hostilities with a view to surrender (Figure 33)—In the meantime, however, we should state that Gen. [Benjamin] Butler had landed with a large force (Figure 34) in the rear of Fort St. Philip,[31] and thus we had them hemmed in on three sides.

On the following day, Monday, April 28th, the forts surrendered to Commodore Porter (Figure 35), and the marines attached to the *Westfield* were ordered to land and take possession of Fort Jackson

FIGURE 35. Refugees from Fort Jackson, April 28, 1862. Sketch No. 20 by Dr. Daniel D. T. Nestell. Courtesy of the Nestell Collection, Nimitz Library, U.S. Naval Academy, Annapolis, Maryland.

(Figure 36)—Fort St. Philip being occupied by men from the other ships. During this time, the other fleet, under Commodore Farragut, had gone up to New Orleans (Figure 37) and taken possession of that city, the forts being the main impediment to that undertaking. And thus, after a siege of nine days, we gained command of the main Southern city and the lower Mississippi, and were ready to enter into another undertaking of equal magnitude.[32] To give an idea of the vastness of our labor, I will copy an estimate made of the number of shells thrown against the forts, and the weight of the iron composing them.[33]

> Shell thrown by mortar fleet, 16,000
> Weight of each, 216 lbs . . . 3,456,000 lbs.
> Shell & shot from the other vessels . . . 250,000 lbs.
> Total weight of iron thrown . . . 3,706,000 lbs.
> Or 1,853 tons

On the 29th we proceeded up to New Orleans (Figure 38), Gen. Butler's troops having been placed in possession of the forts. We remained there until May 1st, when we dropped down to Pilot Town, where we lay over night, and then proceeded down to the bar at the mouth of the river. From there we steamed up again on the 4th (as before mentioned under that date,) for the purpose of extricating one of the bomb schooners from a difficulty into which she had

FIGURE 36. A Casemate at Fort Jackson. Sketch No. 17 by Dr. Daniel D. T. Nestell. Courtesy of the Nestell Collection, Nimitz Library, U.S. Naval Academy, Annapolis, Maryland.

FIGURE 37. Arrival of U.S.S. *Hartford* off New Orleans. Sketch No. 23 by Dr. Daniel D. T. Nestell. Courtesy of the Nestell Collection, Nimitz Library, U.S. Naval Academy, Annapolis, Maryland.

FIGURE 38. Appearance of the Levee at New Orleans. U.S.S. *Clifton* at Left Center. Sketch No. 24 by Dr. Daniel D. T. Nestell. Courtesy of the Nestell Collection, Nimitz Library, U.S. Naval Academy, Annapolis, Maryland.

FIGURE 39. The Landing of Union Troops at Ship Island—1862. From *Harper's Weekly*.

fallen. This occupied us the better part of the day, and in the evening we returned to our anchorage. The next morning the entire bomb fleet set sail for Ship Island, Miss., where we arrived the same night, and where we shall remain at least one day to take in coal (Figure 39).

[At this point, Gusley has completed describing the events up to the time of the commencement of his Note-Book. From this point forward, his entries are made on or within a few days following the events described.—Ed.]

# 2 Ship Island, the Pearl River, and Lake Pontchartrain

We have just anchored off the forts at the entrance to Mobile bay. As I suspected in writing the last page, we remained at Ship Island yesterday for coal,[1] and this morning steamed up the Gulf for this place. Four other steamers accompanied us—the *Harriet Lane* (flag ship), *Clifton*, *Jackson*, and *Miami*.[2] As we approached [Mobile] bay, we saw three of the enemy's gunboats outside the forts. We immediately gave chase and beat to quarters (Figure 40), hoping to come up with and engage them, but they showed us a clean pair of heels and ran in behind the forts. The forts are two in number, Fort Gaines and Fort Morgan,[3] and appear to be very heavy affairs (Figure 41). But we will not anticipate, save to say that we are on the eve of another battle, and to hope that the same success may attend us as at Forts Jackson and St. Philip.

---

We are again at Ship Island. Our stay at Mobile[4] was not so protracted as we were led to believe at first it would be, nor did the battle we anticipated take place.[5] We blockaded the place for two days, and made a reconnaissance, during which the *Clifton* got aground within range of the forts and was fired at quite briskly. She got herself off, however, after being fast about eight hours, without sustaining any damage.[6] On the morning of the 9th, at daylight, a schooner was discovered bound up the bay, between us and the forts, having run the blockade during the night.[7] We all felt somewhat "cheap" on seeing this, but it was too late to overhaul her, and so we did not molest her. Soon after, the Commodore made signals for us to proceed to this place [Ship Island], which

we accordingly did, and arrived here the same afternoon. On our passage up, we passed the ship *Eliza and Ella*, with signals of distress flying. We hailed her, when she answered that she was in a sinking condition, having five feet of water in her hold and gaining on the pumps. There being no immediate danger, and being near the island, we did not go on board, but ordered her to make for this place [Ship Island], where she arrived a few hours after us. We also proved during this passage that of the three sister [ferry] boats (the *Westfield*, *Clifton* and *Jackson*), ours [*Westfield*] was the swiftest vessel.

<hr />

MAY 14, 1862      Yesterday we left Ship Island for Lake Pontchartrain, and proceeded slowly up the outlet, arriving at Madisonville, [Louisiana][8] (Figure 42) about 7 o'clock in the evening. On the way up we overhauled several schooners and a steamer, but all being right we did not detain them.[9] We were also saluted by the Union troops from Fort Pike (Figure 43)[10] at the

FIGURE 42. The Landing at Madisonville, Louisiana. From *Harper's Weekly*.

FIGURE 43. Fort Pike and Lake Pontchartrain, Louisiana. Sketch No. 67 by Dr. Daniel D. T. Nestell. Courtesy of the Nestell Collection, Nimitz Library, U.S. Naval Academy, Annapolis, Maryland.

entrance to the lake. Today we are returning. Nothing of any note has transpired within the last few days. We have rumors of the evacuation of Pensacola by the rebels and the surrender of Mobile. We have plenty of time to fish, and in the evening all hands are piped overboard for a swim.

MAY 21, 1862  Again at Ship Island (Figure 44), which for want of a solid basis we should have ere this described; but whose snow-white sands, and the absence of verdure and trees can easily be recalled without reference to a log-book.[11] And besides, the perspective scenery of the island itself and the harbor, are but transient; and when we shall read this memento of our pastime in our own home, the white tents of the soldiers shall have vanished, and the immense navy riding for the last six months in its surrounding waters will no longer be seen. Under the date of the 14th we stated that we were returning from Lake Pontchartrain. On the evening of that day we anchored off the mouth of Pearl River, a narrow but deep stream, emptying into the Rigolettes,[12] or outlet of the Lake (Figure 45). The next morning we, in conjunction with the gunboats *Sachem* and *Clifton*, proceeded up this river in search of the rebel steamers which we heard had run up there to elude us. The trip was a very pleasant one, and the beautiful scenery and pure fresh air wafted through the

FIGURE 44. Ship Island. Military Scene Showing *Westfield* and *Clifton* in Harbor Near Fort (Left), Troops (Center), and Cavalry (Right). Sketch No. 66 by Dr. Daniel D. T. Nestell. Courtesy of the Nestell Collection, Nimitz Library, U.S. Naval Academy, Annapolis, Maryland.

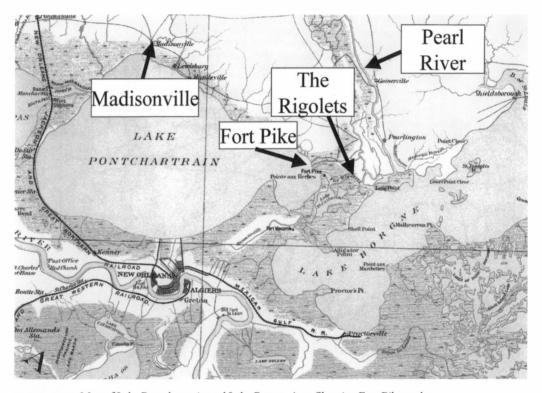

FIGURE 45. Map of Lake Pontchartrain and Lake Borgne Area Showing Fort Pike at the Mouth of the Rigolets Passage Connecting the Lakes. Identification Boxes Added by Editor. From the *OR Atlas*, Plate 156.

trees which lined the river's banks [and] were indeed a treat to us. The river is a very tortuous one, and appears to abound with alligators (Figure 46). The surrounding woods, too, are only beautiful to the sight, the enjoyment of a rest in their shade being rendered extremely dangerous by the presence of innumerable lizards and venomous snakes.

We proceeded up [the Pearl River] about seventy miles, when we found it impossible to double the sharp curves of the river with our vessel. The *Sachem* (Figure 47), however, went on about five miles farther when she was fired upon from the bushes.[13] She returned the fire with grape and canister, but being unable to see the foe, and there being no room to work the vessel, she retired, with two men wounded.[14] Our Captain and a boat's crew from our vessel accompanied her up. In the afternoon we all steamed down the river again, and late at night anchored in Lake Borgne, at the outlet of the Rigolettes. In the morning we found that we were aground; but we soon extricated ourselves from this predicament. While lying aground, our armorer (Jacob Snukel) threw himself overboard and was drowned. No cause is assigned for this rash act, but it is

FIGURE 46. A Graveyard on Pearl River, Mississippi, May 1862, Showing Alligator at Lower Right. Sketch No. 29a by Dr. Daniel D. T. Nestell. Courtesy of the Nestell Collection, Nimitz Library, U.S. Naval Academy, Annapolis, Maryland.

FIGURE 47. U.S. Surveying Steamer *Sachem*. Sketch No. 29b by Dr. Daniel D. T. Nestell. Courtesy of the Nestell Collection, Nimitz Library, U.S. Naval Academy, Annapolis, Maryland.

supposed that he must have become insane. We searched a long time for his body, but could not find it. The same evening (16th) we made Ship Island, and we have laid here ever since. A mail was here for our ship, among which was a letter and some papers from home for me. On the 17th the gunboat *Octorara*[15] came here and the Commodore removed his flag from the *Harriet Lane* to her. Everything is quiet, and rumors are rife that we will be home by July.

# 3 Pensacola

JUNE 1, 1862 Time appears to move on with an amazing swiftness, and the different periods of time change names with a rapidity which almost puzzles one so isolated from newspapers and almanacs to remember. The feeling of being a recruit has to us gradually and imperceptibly passed away, and here in the tag end of the eighth month of our enlistment, we can boast of feeling like an old soldier. We feel, however, that a sufficient time has not yet elapsed for us to review and comment upon our past experience and to make up our mind as to our future plans in regard to re-enlistment. We will note here, however, that notwithstanding we can easily content ourselves to put in the remainder of our full term (and should the war last that long we should not think of doing anything else), yet we would not dream of refusing a proffered honorable discharge at any time prior to that date which the Government might choose to offer one. Even in these stirring times the life of a marine is very monotonous, and judging from this, it must be next to unbearable in time of peace. Events of any note are of so rare occurrence that it is almost useless to waste paper on a Note-Book to record them; and we find that the only way to fill up pages is to adopt a gossiping style, without having anything in view but to perhaps improve our writing and maintain our knowledge of orthography [writing] in order that our hand may not be entirely "out" when we again take up the stick and rule.[1]

Today we are lying at the Pensacola navy-yard (Figure 48), or rather, where it used to be. We arrived here yesterday morning (31st May). On the 28th of May, while yet at Ship Island, we received a mail from the North, in which was a letter for us—which we answered as usual and also wrote one to an old friend in Lancaster. Fresh beef and a fresh

FIGURE 48. Panoramic View of the Pensacola Navy Yard. From David Porter's *Naval History of the Civil War*.

FIGURE 49. Union Fleet Bombarding Fort Morgan. From *Harper's Weekly*.

vegetable soup, the usual delicacies we enjoy upon the arrival of the storeship, was another marked circumstance of this date.

On the 30th we weighed anchor for this place, and had an incident on the way. We stopped about an hour at the mouth of Mobile bay, and fired some eight or ten shots apiece at Fort Morgan with our heavy guns (Figure 49). This was stated to be for the purpose of getting the range for our mortar vessels. The fort returned one shot—a blank cartridge. Some of us thought this was a good joke; but we did not notice any of those who judged the long range of our guns smiling at it. There is no doubt, however, that they will have occasion ere long to fire something more than blanks at us, and will do so if they are not as timid here as they were at Pensacola.[2] It will require a far better joke than that to cover up the atrocities they committed here. A heap of smoldering ruins is all that can now be seen of the once beautiful town of Warrington and one of the finest navy yards owned by the United States. There are three fine forts guarding the mouth of the harbor (Figure 50), two of which were in the possession of the *cavalry*; yet they were too cowardly to risk the issue of an honorable battle, and they sneaked off and burned and

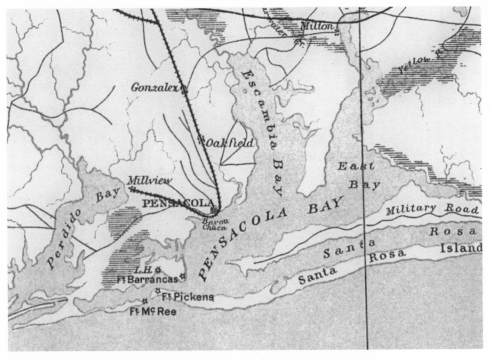

FIGURE 50. Pensacola Bay and the Forts (Lower Left) Guarding the Main Entrance to the Bay. From the *OR Atlas*, Plate 147.

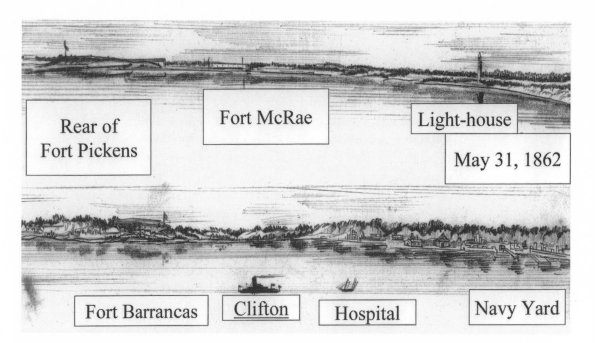

Rear of
Fort Pickens

Fort McRae

Light-house

May 31, 1862

Fort Barrancas

Clifton

Hospital

Navy Yard

FIGURE 51. Panoramic View of Pensacola Bay Looking South (Upper Register) and North (Bottom Register) from *Clifton*'s Position in the Bay. May 31, 1862. Sketch No. 33 by Dr. Daniel D. T. Nestell. Caption Boxes Added By Editor Replace Same Text Handwritten By Nestell. Courtesy of the Nestell Collection, Nimitz Library, U.S. Naval Academy, Annapolis, Maryland.

FIGURE 52. The Great Water Spout off "Round Island" in Mississippi Sound. Sketch No. 30 by Dr. Daniel D. T. Nestell. Courtesy of the Nestell Collection, Nimitz Library, U.S. Naval Academy, Annapolis, Maryland.

destroyed everything in the shape of barracks, hospitals, etc. I predict that the next time they attempt to take [Forts] McRae [McRee] or Barrancas (Figure 51), they will have to perform some more chivalric act than smiting a single, hoary-headed quartermaster, and conquering a dozen marines.[3]

We saw two waterspouts (Figure 52) today in the Gulf, across Santa Rosa Island.

—◦◦◦—

JUNE 4, 1862    Today we are on our way to New Orleans. We steamed up the river from Warrington on Monday for the city of Pensacola, a distance of ten miles, and had a fine sight of the city and the spacious bay (Figure 53). We returned the same evening, but soon, in conjunction with the other steamers of the fleet, went up again. Of course we all anticipated a fine time going ashore; but of course we didn't have the said fine time. Some of our sailors who were ashore at Warrington were blamed for some misdemeanors committed there, and so the entire fleet were restricted of liberty by an order from the commander of the land forces.[4] What a commentary might here be made upon the innocent being compelled to suffer for the guilty, or rather with them. But we refrain, lest it might be thought that we were very much chagrined at this restriction. Yesterday afternoon the entire mortar fleet left Warrington. Our

FIGURE 53. Pensacola, Florida. Sketch No. 34 by Dr. Daniel D. T. Nestell. Courtesy of the Nestell Collection, Nimitz Library, U. S. Naval Academy, Annapolis, Maryland.

vessel, being short of coal, remained until 10 o'clock last night taking in a supply, when we steamed out of the bay and into the broad gulf in the track of our fellow travelers. As yet we have not overhauled any of them, and we are in sight of land near the mouths of the Mississippi.

———— ❦ ————

JUNE 5, 1862    We do not wish to make a daily task of this memorandum keeping, but the extreme heat of the place we are now lying at has such a *stirring* effect, both in its own temperature and the animation it gives to the countless swarms of flies that have taken up their habitation in our vessel, that we find it impossible on the one hand to allow our mind to be idle and thus more keenly feel the rays of Sol, and on the other hand to allow both mind and body to attempt the refreshing process of a doze, thereby running the risk of being brought to full wakefulness a dozen times or so with an unconscious (but equally culpable) profane expression on our lips in condemnation of these active little insects. Therefore we will indite[5] another page to our Note-Book, and if not already comprehended as regards the state of the atmosphere here, we will state that we remember once reading, in one of the lives of the gulf pirates of yore, the expressions of a fat Dutch mate among them on this head[ing], when once on a time his vessel was becalmed in these latitudes. "Dunder and blitzen," said he, "I do pelieve dat hell ish rite benunder dis Gulf of Mexico." At least we know that no other furnace would be hot enough to impart the degree of warmth felt here at present.

Shortly after leaving off our writing yesterday, we had the pleasure of seeing ourselves pass into Mississippi water, although we are yet anchored in the gulf. For the distance of about two miles from its mouth, the water of the river refuses to mingle with those of the gulf, and at that point one can with one hand dip up a vessel of green salt water and with the other one of fresh muddy water. The line of demarcation is plainly seen even at a great distance, and crossing it one feels at least as if he had seen one of the wonders of nature. When we arrived here (Passe a l'Outre) we found the *Octorara* (flag ship), *Jackson*, and *Miami* anchored. We passed the *Owasco* about two miles out, and the *Clifton* had stopped at Mobile which we heard had been evacuated and set on fire.[6] Altogether we had a pleasant trip here and we found on comparing with our consorts that our vessel had made the quickest time by two hours. The flag ship proceeded up the river to New Orleans as soon as we hove in sight, and the *Westfield* is flag ship until we rejoin her.

# 4 New Orleans

We have to record today the fact that we are once more at Pilot Town, on the Mississippi river, or, rather, the South West pass of that river. On a former occasion we have noticed this town (Figure 54), and the only alteration now perceptible is that there is a hospital established here for the benefit of the fleet now on the river. We ran here yesterday for the purpose of coaling, and landed one of our officers who was sick of a fever. On the 6th of June a stiff breeze sprung up, the mortar schooners hove in sight at Passe a l'Outre, and some of them proceeded up above. By evening all were in, and we took a tow of two and proceeded up to New Orleans. We passed Forts Jackson and St. Philip about ten o'clock the same night and were hailed—but not in the same manner as on a previous occasion.[1] When near the city one of our

FIGURE 54. Pilot Town, Louisiana—1862. From *Harper's Weekly*.

tow parted her cable, and in endeavoring to make her fast again she ran ashore where we left her and proceeded up with the remaining one. We arrived at New Orleans on the afternoon of the 7th, and anchored astern of the Commodore. A traitor by the name of Wm. Mumford was suspended from the top of the U.S. customhouse [Mint][2] (Figure 55) when we arrived, having been hung that day by order of Gen. Butler, for tearing down the American flag which had been raised on the building on the entrance of our troops in that city. We found the city somewhat changed since we were last there. The streets were no longer deserted, but wore the appearance of a brisk re-opening of business, and the docks (Figure 56) were almost filled with shipping. On our way up, also, we passed scores of merchant vessels bound for the city. Yesterday (8th) it being understood that we were to proceed up the river to Vicksburg, we dropped down the river to this place [Pilot Town] for the purpose of taking in a sufficiency of coal for the trip. We made the passage down in eight hours. The distance is 120 miles.

FIGURE 55. The Mint in New Orleans, Louisiana. From *Butler's Book*, vol. 1.

FIGURE 56. The Levee at New Orleans, Louisiana. From *Butler's Book*, vol. 1.

JUNE 12, 1862     That we are again lying off New Orleans (Figure 57) is about all that we can note down under this date. A description of the city by us would have to be founded on mere supposition, and might perhaps be a recapitulation of standard geographical descriptions, and therefore be deemed plagiarism; or by relying on the tales of others, perhaps we might indite something which would be as full of fiction as the game of "perhaps" told by a Mississippi steamboat captain to Madam Trollope, in order to rid himself of her continued and vexatious inquiries after information as to the "manners and customs of Americans."[3] To make ourself more perfectly understood, we will say that although we have been anchored here since the evening of the 10th, yet we have had no privilege of visiting the city, nor do we expect any if we lay here for a month. Forgetfulness on the part of our captain, or a total disregard for the welfare (not to hint at the pleasure) of the men, keeps us all on board. It seems hard, very hard, to some of us; but it's fair, we suppose, and so we drop the subject. Still it would appear to us much fairer and far more pleasant were he to open his heart and our "prison-doors" and cite with slight alterations to suit the occasion, the well known refrain:

FIGURE 57. Panoramic View of Union Ships Anchored in the Mississippi River off New Orleans (1862). From *The Soldier in Our Civil War*, vol. 1.

> Open thy wings, sweet bird, and be thou free;
> Thy prison doors I open wide;
> There's room enough outside for you and me;
> And all the world beside!

Last night, while on post from 10 to 12, we had the liberty of seeing a total eclipse of the moon. This, no doubt, might have been seen elsewhere. This morning we saw a party of boys drown a dog in the dock.

# 5 The Mississippi River

JUNE 19, 1862 Transitory, indeed, is our present life. Each succeeding twenty-four hours finds us at a different place. Last Friday we, in conjunction with the rest of the steamers of the fleet, started up the Mississippi river for Vicksburg, each with a tow of two mortar schooners; and today we find ourselves in the vicinity of Rodney, Miss., which is said to be sixty miles from the place of our destination. The maps will show that we have passed many towns, both small and large, on our way up; but a description of them by one who merely passes them by in a steamer is impossible. We can only say of the majority of them that they are beautifully situated on bends of the river, near the bluffs which occasionally occur along its banks, and which serve as an invincible levee to them in cases of the frequent overflowings of the river. There is a picturesqueness about them that leads a passer by to suppose that they are pleasant places to live in, and the trees which line their streets add much to their beauty and unquestionably to their comfort. Besides these numerous towns the shores on both sides of the river are lined with beautiful plantations. From New Orleans to Baton Rouge they seem like one continued city, and their thriving lands and beautiful levees mark it as one of the most desirable places for one to lead a happy life. The much talked of hardships of the Southern slave have been to us proven a chimera by this trip up the great Mississippi through the hot-bed of slavery. We have had occasion to notice these "down-trodden human beings" in some of the phases of their servitude. At morn, at noon, at night, on Sundays and on week days we have seen them; and their appearance and demeanor when placed beside the same merits of us man-o'-wars-men appeared to equal if not exceed ours. Often we have been

FIGURE 58. Ellis' Cliff. From *Harper's Weekly*.

astir for hours before we saw them go to their tasks; we have been
denied the privilege of leaning upon or touching the railing of the
ship in order to get a better view of the surrounding scenery, when
at the same time we have seen them cease work for a half hour and
lean upon their hoes and shovels to admire the Yankee ships. We
have noticed them at evening sporting around their neat cabins, their
rude singing proclaiming them happy, whilst our masters proclaimed
"silence" in the places boasting the most freedom on our vessel.
And we have everywhere noticed that Sunday is a universal holiday
among them. Their condition as compared with the free Negro of
the North is a Paradise. Philanthropy, if practiced among those
near them, instead of being extended only where the most notoriety
is supposed to be gained by it, might be a virtue in some of our
Northern leaders.

Our passage up this river is necessarily slow, owing to the swift
current we have to stem. Besides this, being in an enemy's country we
use the precaution to proceed only in the day time. Night before last,
just after sundown, we were fired upon from Ellis' Bluff (Figure 58),[1]
below Natchez. We threw a few shell on the bluff, and soon silenced
that kind of sport.[2] A pet dog on board the *Owasco* is the only loss
we sustained on our side.[3] One of our shells set a house near the
bluff on fire, and unless our assailants were pretty well scattered

it is reasonable to suppose that some one was hurt. Last evening we raked the bushes on the Mississippi shore with grape and canister before anchoring, and all was quiet throughout the night.

———◦———

**JUNE 24, 1862**    Lying off Vicksburg, Miss.[4] (Figure 59) with the thermometer at 95 [degrees] in the shade, and with nothing else to do, we have seated ourselves to add another page or so to our Note-Book. We arrived at our present anchorage on the evening of the 20th, without being further molested on our way [other] than mentioned under our last date. We found part of Com. Farragut's fleet (Figure 60) at anchor, which had been investing the town for some days before our arrival. On Saturday, (21st) some of our mortar boats tried the range of their bombs on a battery between us and the town and were briskly answered for a time; but they soon silenced the battery and ceased firing.[5] Contrabands have been coming off from the town and the plantations in its vicinity ever since our arrival here. We pitched a large tent for them on an island in the river, under the guns of the shipping, and have already a colony of some fifty or sixty, of all sizes and colors (Figure 61).[6]

On Sunday afternoon the balance of our mortars arrived, in tow of two Mississippi steamers. With them came a communication for the Commodore, from the Secretary of the Navy, thanking him and the officers and seamen and marines under his command for their gallantry in the bombardment of Forts Jackson and St. Philip.

FIGURE 59. Detail from View of the "Grand Assault" on Vicksburg. June 22, 1862, Showing *Westfield* (W) at Bottom Left and *Clifton* (C) at Center Left. Sketch No. 37 by Dr. Daniel D. T. Nestell. Courtesy of the Nestell Collection, Nimitz Library, U.S. Naval Academy, Annapolis, Maryland.

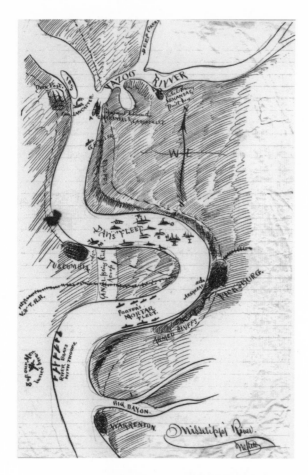

FIGURE 60. Vicksburg and the Union Fleet. Sketch No. 35 by Dr. Daniel D. T. Nestell. Courtesy of the Nestell Collection, Nimitz Library, U.S. Naval Academy, Annapolis, Maryland.

FIGURE 61. Contraband Camp, Formerly Used as a Female Seminary. G. H. Suydam Collection, Mss. 1394, Louisiana and Lower Mississippi Valley Collections, LSU Libraries, Louisiana State University, Baton Rouge, Louisiana.

All hands were mustered on board the *Westfield*, and the document read to us by our Captain.[7] That it was a happy day for all hands, and the proudest moment of our individual life, it is needless to here record. History may record the gallant deeds of our navy, and many may be alive to read with unfeigned pleasure of the terrible times in which they bore a part. But far greater is the pleasure of being called together for the purpose of receiving the written thanks of your country, while yet those deeds are fresh in your memory.

Yesterday evening some stir was caused among the fleet by the appearance of a large raft bearing down upon us. We at first thought of all kinds of infernal machines[8] and Secesh[9] tricks, but these were quickly dispelled by the recurrence of the fact that the river had risen somewhat during the night, and it became clear to us that the said raft had broken loose somewhere up the river. The *Jackson* towed it ashore.

➤◦◄

**JULY 1, 1862**   Still off Vicksburg; and, we might add, we are perfectly satisfied that we are in the same position as at our last writing. That we have attempted to advance our position and to occupy the town is the prominent item we have to note. On the morning of the 26th we placed our bombers [mortar schooners] in position, and at daylight opened on the batteries near to the

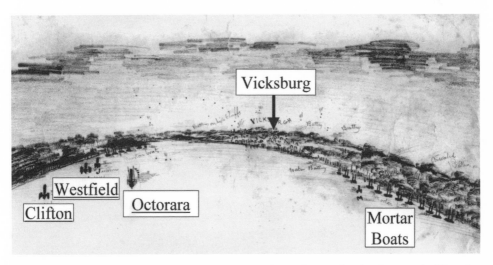

FIGURE 62. Attack on Vicksburg, June 27, by the Mortar Fleet Under the Command of David Porter, the Sloops-of-War Lying 5 Miles Down the River. Identification Boxes Added by Editor to Replace Same Text Handwritten by Nestell. Sketch No. 39 by Dr. Daniel D. T. Nestell. Courtesy of the Nestell Collection, Nimitz Library, U.S. Naval Academy, Annapolis, Maryland.

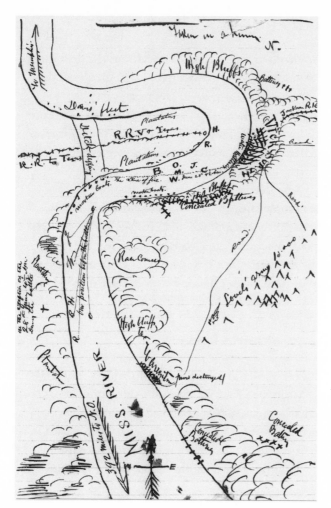

FIGURE 63. The Battle Before Vicksburg, Mississippi, June 28, 1862. Sketch No. 40 by Dr. Daniel D. T. Nestell. Courtesy of the Nestell Collection, Nimitz Library, U.S. Naval Academy, Annapolis, Maryland.

FIGURE 64. The Grave of the First Slain on Board the U.S. Steamer *Clifton*, at the Bombardment of Vicksburg, Mississippi, June 28, on the Mississippi River 2 Miles Below Vicksburg. Sketch No. 42 by Dr. Daniel D. T. Nestell. Courtesy of the Nestell Collection, Nimitz Library, U.S. Naval Academy, Annapolis, Maryland.

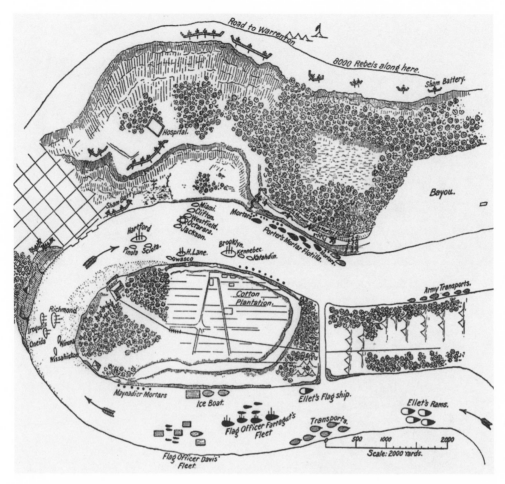

FIGURE 65. Chart Showing the Position of the U.S. Force Before Vicksburg up Until the 10th of July, 1862. ORN, vol. 18.

town. They answered us briskly throughout the day, but did us no damage.[10] The next day we continued the fire (Figure 62), and on Saturday morning [June 28] about four o'clock the steamers made an assault on the town and the batteries. The battle (Figure 63) lasted over two hours, and was a terrible affair, but none of the rebel batteries were silenced.[11]

Part of the steamers passed the town and the remainder retired to their anchorage.[12] The fight was equally as terrible as the one at Forts Jackson and Saint Philip, and far more destructive to our fleet. The *Jackson* had one man killed; the *Clifton* received a shot through her boilers, and had eight killed (Figure 64) and several scalded; and our own vessel [*Westfield*] received a large rifle shot through her wheel and within an ace of her steam-chest.[13] One of our marines picked

FIGURE 66. "Attack Upon the Mortar-Fleet By Rebel Land Forces." From *Harper's Weekly*.

FIGURE 67. "A Secesh Soldier from Vicksburg." Sketch No. 36 by Dr. Daniel D. T. Nestell. Courtesy of the Nestell Collection, Nimitz Library, U.S. Naval Academy, Annapolis, Maryland.

up the shot while yet rolling across the deck, and we have it on board as a trophy. We kept up a fire from the bomb schooners throughout the day, which was answered by the rebels at intervals (Figure 65). On Sunday we lay quiet until noon, when the batteries opened on us again, which we returned from all our mortars, and soon made them desist.

The same programme was performed on Monday, the only variation being that in the evening we observed two [Confederate] regiments leaving the town and marching for the ships, through the woods which line the banks of the river (Figure 66). Our pickets were driven in, and the ships raked the woods with grape and shell, which had the effect of making them "skedaddle." Some of their men got stuck in a swamp in their hurry to get out of the reach of our artillery, and our pickets on advancing again took three prisoners. Two of them (Figure 67) were brought on board the *Westfield*. They were covered with mud and dirt, but our tars soon metamorphosed them into clean, tidy-looking sailors. They gave some valuable information as to the position and strength of the rebels. They are Tennesseans.[14]

———— >☾< ————

JULY 10, 1862 The writer under our last date was suddenly drawn to a close by an order for the marines to get ready to land. Although knowing that our purpose in going ashore was not for pleasure, and being aware of going in rather dangerous proximity of very rabid rebels, yet it was to all of us a very acceptable order, and in a trice we were all armed, equipped and waiting.[15] That great and glorious deeds were by us performed while on shore, that batteries innumerable were taken at the point of the bayonet by the invincible marines, or that Vicksburg, that frowning city which has so long separated us from the upper flotilla of the Mississippi, is ours, we cannot chronicle: that we would like to record such facts we cannot deny; and that we expected, if ever it would be our lot to again open this our Note-Book, to do so, we plead guilty. Last evening we were ordered aboard our respective vessels, and today the rumor is rife that we are to proceed down the river to New Orleans, and in confirmation of the rumors our mortar vessels have been taken in tow by the steamers, and we are now lying by apparently for a fair start. If we may believe the rumors as to why this immense naval demonstration of ours is to end in the fizzle now so apparent, we may with great confidence here record the fact that the military and naval operations in this rebellion are meted out to aspirants or claimants in the same manner as other political spoils of the Administration. *Vide*: One Commodore, with a powerful fleet of steamers, proceeds victoriously up the river to this place and demands the surrender of the only remaining stronghold of secession on the Mississippi. The answer he receives is, "Come and take it."[16] He comes; he tries; but he don't take it. Another and a more powerful fleet, consisting of twenty mortar vessels and seven steamers, is called on to aid the first. For six days the combined fleets invest the city, and in the grand final trial they are both worsted. Land forces, belonging to the fleet, then arrive from below, and preparations for another and greater effort are made. In the meantime the upper flotilla from Island No. 10 and Memphis arrives, and in the rumored altercation as to the right of one party to reduce the place in preference to the other, hostilities cease—our three fleets lie idle—and the rebels are busily engaged in reinforcing themselves, and strengthening and extending their fortifications. Now the most powerful and efficient portion of the expedition is ordered off, and the weakest (numerically speaking) portion left to contend with a more powerful adversary than defied us all combined. This is a strange proceeding. "Them's my sentiments," as the hoosier said when he had expressed himself on the tariff question. But we hope, like him, to see in the end that it was all for the best; adding however that there must be a very small loss of life to make us confess to it.

Our last week's experience in soldiering has made us feel somewhat proud of the wisdom we displayed when we ignored the volunteer [army] corps and pitched upon the navy as the place in which to show our devotion to our country. We then had an idea of the hardships of camp-life, we now have had the experience of it; and we may add, that although our idea was nearly up to the mark, yet our experience added somewhat to it. We had plenty of picket duty (which, by the way, includes the hardest part of a soldier's life), a few skirmishes and a reunion with some old friends.

———◦———

JULY 25, 1862   This morning we are en route for New Orleans, and have just passed Grand Gulf (Figure 68),[17] where we were much disappointed at not being attacked by the rebels, who had been molesting all our vessels at this point since we passed up. The town we found to be entirely burned. From the time of our last writing until the 15th, the siege of Vicksburg was carried on in a slow and ineffective manner. On the evening of that day a

FIGURE 68. "Running the Grand Gulf—Found it Burned by Our Boats Coming Up, July 11, 1862." Sketch No. 44 by Dr. Daniel D. T. Nestell. Courtesy of the Nestell Collection, Nimitz Library, U.S. Naval Academy, Annapolis, Maryland.

FIGURE 69. "The Rebel Ram *Arkansas* Running Through the Union Fleet off Vicksburg." From *Harper's Weekly*.

rebel ram made its way through the upper fleet and anchored off the town, which event caused quite a stir among our fleet (Figure 69).[18] One of our mortar schooners which had become aground was set on fire and blown up,[19] and the remainder dropped down, while the steamers were got under way and ready for action. At dark the upper fleets made a combined attack on the city, and our fleet went up to assist, taking the bombers along. After a battle of over two hours we silenced their batteries and fired the town. After the battle Com. Farragut's fleet remained below, together with two of Com. [Charles H.] Davis' fleet.[20] Nothing of importance has occurred from that [day] to this, save to note that the health of the fleet is very bad.

———◦———

**AUGUST 3, 1862**    We are again lying off New Orleans, after having been on the move ever since our last writing. On the evening of that day we anchored in the river at Ellis Cliff, where we lay until next morning, in order to see our transports safely by that suspicious place. As at Grand Gulf, we were not molested, although we expected an attack there. We had a remarkably pleasant trip from the Cliff to the city [of New Orleans] (Figure 70), where we arrived the same afternoon, the 26th. We found a large mail awaiting us here, which had accumulated during our stay at Vicksburg. Four letters and a half dozen papers (Figure 71) fell to our share, which it would be superfluous to say were gladly received. Item: We answered them next day. We lay at New Orleans until Thursday [July 31], when we took a tow of three bombers and proceeded to the mouth of Passe a l'Outre, where we arrived the next morning. We returned through the South West Pass, and stopped at Pilot Town for the purpose of taking in a supply of coal. This occupied the whole day, and the next morning (yesterday) we proceeded on our way up to New Orleans, arriving there in the cool of the evening.

This moving around and getting a snuff of Gulf air appears to have a salutary effect upon all hands. The sick have all suddenly become well, and those who were incurable have been sent home; and the old *Westfield* looks as spry and lively as she did when we first visited this city. The [Mississippi] river has fallen a great deal since we first entered it, and the scenery along its banks is much improved by this fact. Plantations which appeared beautiful to us on our former passages, notwithstanding they seemed to be floating residences, are now, with their high, green levees, gorgeous to look upon. These sights, coupled with the beautiful skies at sunset, makes the passage

FIGURE 70.
Panoramic View of
Union Ships Anchored
in the Mississippi
River off New Orleans
(1862). From *The
Soldier in Our Civil
War*, vol. 1

FIGURE 71. "'Tween Decks After Action—News from Home." From *Harper's Weekly*.

of this river a perfect treat. The warm weather and the mosquitoes which we have on former occasions deprecated, have both decreased—the one in temperature and the other in numbers. Gallynippers (a cross between a horse-fly and a hornet) it is true have paid us a transient visit, but they have disappeared. I hope they have all been annihilated. This change to a passable degree of comfort is attributable to the refreshing showers, which are of almost daily occurrence here. May they continue until cold weather reigns supreme.

# 6 Baton Rouge, Plaquemine, and Donaldsonville

AUGUST 7, 1862   We had hoped and came near so announcing at our last writing, that our next penning of notes would be done at Pensacola; but such are the sudden changes in these war times that we are compelled to date this page at Baton Rouge, La. (Figure 72). Besides noting this sudden change in the programme of our expectations, we have to note what we have not had occasion to note before, and perhaps what we may not have to note again until another six months have gone by, or until these pages shall have been filled up with remarks on what we may see while on board the *Westfield*. But we will not indulge in such vague anticipations, and thereby delay the naming of this important item, viz: On the 5th inst. [instant] the half of the ship's company to which we are attached were given a day's liberty in New Orleans; and to

FIGURE 72. Baton Rouge, 1862. From *Harper's Weekly*.

say the least of this is to state that we enjoyed the gayest 24 hours since we have been attached to the above-mentioned vessel. Our men all conducted themselves in a manner to warrant a repetition of our commander's kindness; but the action of the rebels at this place [Baton Rouge] hurried us from this city and turned our backs upon another where the same enjoyment could have been had, and even was promised. But as soon as we were all safely aboard, we got under way for this place, and were soon hurrying in the wake of Com. Farragut, who had got under way early in the morning. The cause of this was that word was sent us that the rebels had attacked our troops at Baton Rouge, and in conjunction with the infernal ram [C.S.S. *Arkansas*], which we have before mentioned as forcing a passage through our fleets at Vicksburg, had committed great havoc among them and that they needed reinforcements.[1] We came up with the Commodore about midnight, lying at anchor about thirty miles below, and anchored near him.

This morning early we started on our way again, and at noon dropped our anchor off Baton Rouge (Figure 73). We found two gunboats and about eight or nine transports lying here, and the American flag still flying from the State House (Figure 74). We found also that the report here of the affair that had reached us was by no means exaggerated; but that quite a terrible battle had taken place.[2] An army of about 12,000 rebels, under [Gen. Mansfield] Lovell, attacked our forces (amounting to 5,000) under cover of a thick fog and aided by their ram from the river. After a sharp

FIGURE 73. Baton Rouge, Louisiana, with U.S.S. *Hartford* in Center. Sketch No. 26 by Dr. Daniel D. T. Nestell. Courtesy of the Nestell Collection, Nimitz Library, U.S. Naval Academy, Annapolis, Maryland.

FIGURE 74. State House, Baton Rouge, Louisiana. G. H. Suydam Collection, Mss. 1394, Louisiana and Lower Mississippi Valley Collections, LSU Libraries, Louisiana State University, Baton Rouge, Louisiana.

engagement in which our loss in killed and wounded was 250 and that of the rebels over 800 (mostly left upon the field) our troops succeeded in repulsing the enemy and maintaining possession of the city (Figure 75). At the same time the two gunboats lying here (one the *Kineo*, of Farragut's fleet, and the other the iron-clad steamer *Sumter*, of Davis' fleet) went up to engage the rebel ram [*Arkansas*], and after a short running fight compelled the crew to blow her up to prevent her falling into our hands. The bravery of the land troops in this engagement, as well as of the sailors on the gunboats is very highly praised. No less than six times was the battery of the Wisconsin regiment taken by the enemy and retaken again,[3] the Wisconsin men in the last charge refusing to use anything but the bayonet. But great as the glory won by our boys, they have much to mourn for in the loss of their gallant commander, Brig. Gen. [Thomas] Williams, who fell in the early part of the engagement. Several of his staff were also killed. The rebels also lost three generals, their commander, [Gen. Mansfield] Lovell, having been taken aboard of one [of] our transports about an hour ago, with both legs shot off.[4] He was found upon the field, having been left there by his cowardly followers. Much is said about the perfidy of the rebels in this attack, but we shall wait for confirmation before inditing any more on the subject.

FIGURE 75. Waterfront of Baton Rouge, Louisiana and Steamer *Empire Parrish*. Headquarters of General Banks. G. H. Suydam Collection, Mss. 1394, Louisiana and Lower Mississippi Valley Collections, LSU Libraries, Louisiana State University, Baton Rouge, Louisiana.

**AUGUST 12, 1862** Today we are anchored off the city of Pensacola, Florida. As we have before noticed the city, and as the time is at present precious to us, we will not attempt to add anything to the description we have given of it; but shall merely make up our notes to the present date. On the morning of the 8th we left Baton Rouge, with orders from Com. Farragut to stop at Plaquemine and Donaldsonville, and notify the inhabitants to evacuate the towns, as it was his intention to follow us immediately and burn them, owing to the fact of our transports being continually fired upon from and near the towns. We made all possible haste and soon were at anchor off the former place with our guns cast loose and bearing on the town, and sent a guard of marines on shore to bring off the Mayor, for the purpose of having an interview with him. But his Honor made a hasty retreat on the back of a fleet charger on the lowering of our boat, and in lieu of him some of the principal citizens were brought aboard. They were informed of our errand, and attempted to expostulate; but the orders we had were inexorable. They had been before warned of the fate that awaited the town if our transports were again molested, and their assurances of their innocence and their loyalty to the United States availed nothing. At Donaldsonville the same scene was enacted. We have since learned that the former place was spared for another trial, but the latter was razed to the ground (Figure 76).[5] Barbarous as these proceedings may appear, they are but just in retaliation of the infamous and cowardly acts of the rebels, and no doubt will serve as wholesome warnings to citizens of other towns who aid and abet guerilla parties.[6] The same evening we anchored at a beautiful plantation, about ten miles above the city of New Orleans, for the purpose of procuring some fresh provisions, where we remained until next morning, when we started for the city, arriving there about 9 o'clock. We lay at our old anchorage opposite the "Memphis Packet Landing" until Monday morning, when we started in conjunction with the steamer *Jackson* for this place [Pensacola]. When passing Mobile at 12 o'clock last night, we were, through some misunderstanding in signals, fired upon with shell by the steamer *Susquehanna* of the blockading squadron. Without this, we had a very smooth and pleasant passage, and the blue, clear waters of the Gulf were quite a relief from the muddy waters of the Mississippi river.

FIGURE 76. Donaldsonville, Louisiana, After Bombardment by U.S. Navy, 1862. Courtesy of the Christopher Auger Collection, The Abraham Lincoln Presidential Library and Museum, Springfield, Illinois.

# 7 The Return to Pensacola and Ship Island

**AUGUST 14, 1862** Our advent into Pensacola was marked by a very decided rise in the temperature. The thermometer for the few last days of our stay in the Mississippi ranged low in the 80 [degrees], but we had scarcely passed the forts at the entrance of this capacious and beautiful harbor (Figure 77) when it suddenly rose high among the 90 [degrees], and at noon reached 102 [degrees], which point it kept for several hours during that day, and which it has since attained diurnally. Still the average temperature here appears to be much lower than that around New Orleans, and no degree of heat could make it as unhealthy here as there. There, when the sun had set, a heated fog arose from the river

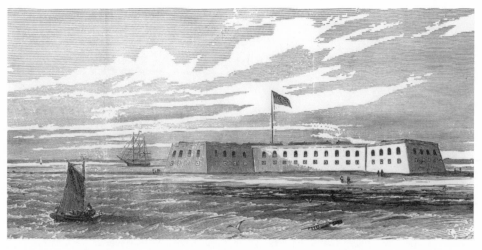

FIGURE 77. Fort Pickens, on Santa Rosa Island, Pensacola Bay, Florida. From *Frank Leslie's Illustrated Famous Leaders and Battle Scenes of the Civil War.*

and the swamps along its banks, which rendered the atmosphere almost stifling; while here that part of the day is truly delightful. A cool breeze from the sea is then felt, which is invariably strong enough to ruffle the smooth waters of the bay, and causing it to emit that peculiar, healthful smell which salt water possesses. In addition to this, we have many cooling showers, and that pest of warm latitude, mosquitoes, are less abundant. Taken as a whole, we consider ourselves fortunate in our last change of position, nor do we wish to risk another before cold weather. To make the place more satisfactory still is the fact of our being allowed more liberty here than could be expected elsewhere on the Gulf station at present. Boats and nets are freely allowed the men, to fish any place in the bay they think fit, and every day we have our turns for a run ashore. True, as yet, fish appear to be scarce, and the dearness of things in the town [Pensacola] and the strict military discipline carried out there prevent one from "going in lemons,"[1] yet the privilege of leaving the ship and doing as you please for ten or twelve hours after being penned up for six months, is sufficient to make a note of. News is not so plent[iful] here as at New Orleans, and surmises as regards the successes of our different armies are, of course, plentiful. Under the head of news we may state that the full particulars of the affair at Baton Rouge has reached us. Our account under date of the 7th is in the main correct. The rebel ram [*Arkansas*] was destroyed, their land forces were defeated, and the number of killed and wounded was correct. They lost three Generals, but the traitor Lovell was not among them. The forces engaged were 6,000 rebels instead of 12,000, as then stated, and 2,500 Federals instead of 5,000. The battle took place on the 5th inst.[2]

———◦◦◦———

AUGUST 22, 1862   Already a marked difference in the temperature is felt here, and a wintry coldness is experienced from midnight till sunrise. This, however, may not prove that all the warm weather has passed, but reminds one forcibly that autumn is fast coming on. The last week has been a remarkably quiet one with us—nothing very noticeable having occurred in the fleet. Last Sunday the *Rhode Island* arrived from New York with a small mail for us. Two others have since reached us from New Orleans, but neither contained anything for *the* us [me]. Dispatches from the Navy Department were the main burden of these mails, in which many radical changes in the navy were noticed, among which was

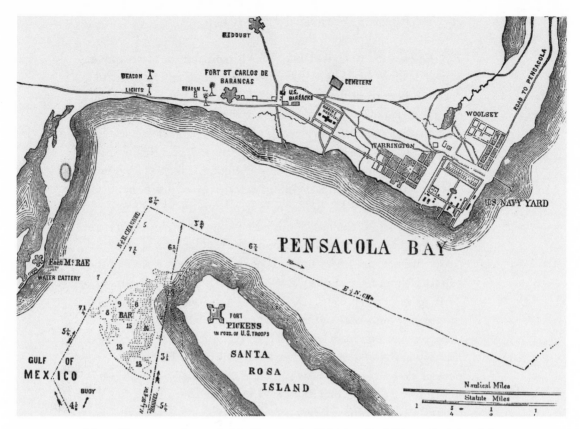

FIGURE 78. Map of Entrance to Pensacola Bay Showing the U.S. Navy Yard (Center Right) and the Forts Built to Defend It. From *The Soldier in Our Civil War*, vol. 1.

the making of numerous Admirals, Commodores, &c., and the stoppage of the spirit ration of seamen, marines, &c. On the 20th, *Admiral Farragut*[3] arrived here in company with the *Brooklyn*, and since then the sloops *Prebel* [*Preble*], *Portsmouth* and *Iroquois* have also arrived. Yesterday the flags were at half mast, and at noon a salute was fired by the Admiral, on the reception of the news of [Former President] Martin Van Buren's death.[4] The day was occupied by us in coaling ship, at Warrington navy yard (Figure 78), where we are now lying.

AUGUST 26, 1862    This morning we left our anchorage off the city of Pensacola, and steamed down the bay for the navy yard, where we have just anchored. We left this place late in the evening of the date of our last writing for Pensacola, where we have since laid, and where we enjoyed the privileges mentioned in our last notice of that city. We availed ourself of the privilege of going ashore over night, notwithstanding the utter

emptiness of our purse, and we must say we will never commit such
a gross mistake again. An all night's rain added to our misery, and the
only pleasure we experienced was the meeting of an old friend from
New York, belonging to Wilson's Zouaves (6th N.Y.V.)[5]

On the 23d, the Admiral [Farragut] came up to the city from
the navy yard in the steamer *Albatross*, and was saluted with thirteen guns from the *Vincennes* and thirteen from the shore when he
landed. He returned the same evening. The weather still continues
comfortably cool, with almost daily showers, and rumors as to our
going home and not going are exceeding rife. A rumor has reached
us that Baton Rouge has been seized by the rebels and burned,[6] but
it needs confirmation. The troops in and around Pensacola, we learn,
have been transferred to Gen. Butler's division from Gen. Hunter's.

———◦◦———

**AUGUST 31, 1862**   "Pleasant weather, with moderate breezes
from the north-east," is the sole amount
of the remarks on the ship's logs now-a-days. A variation from this
routine was, however, made yesterday, or rather an addition to it, in
the noticing of the arrival of the frigates *Potomac* and *Susquehanna*,
the gunboats *Kennebec* and *Kanahwa*, and the mail steamers *Rhode
Island* and *Ocean Queen*.[7] These war vessels make quite an addition to the already large fleet here, and the harbor presents a very
warlike appearance. The news brought by the mail steamers was very
meager and unimportant and the letters so scarce that we did not
get a share of them. Yesterday afternoon we steamed up to the city
[of Pensacola] again, where we are now lying. The city, of course,
presents the same dull appearance as on our former visits, and we
all expect another run ashore. Some of the troops, we learn, are to
be transferred by Gen. Butler from here to New Orleans, which will
make the place still less lively. We might also notice in our log the
appearance for the past week of a bright comet in the firmament
coursed N.W. by N., as the sailors say.[8] Today being Sunday, we had
divine services as usual, and in addition we had read to us the official
thanks of Congress, through Admiral Farragut, for our gallantry
in the reduction of Forts Jackson and St. Philip and the capture of
New Orleans.[9] Under date of June 24th we noticed the fact of having
received thanks for the same affair; but on reference we see that was
from the Secretary of the Navy, whereas this is from Congress. This
document was acceptable if for no other reason merely because it
acted as an offset to the one that followed it in relation to the stop-

FIGURE 79. "Splicing the Main Brace for the Last Time in the U.S. Navy, September 30, 1862." Drawing by Charles Ellery Stedman, Surgeon, "On the Blockade" Sketchbook, Stedman Collection, Courtesy of the Boston Athenaeum.

page of the spirit ration (Figure 79).[10] Demonstrations pro or con upon the reading of either were not indulged in, and, indeed, are not allowed; but that much was and is thought upon them (especially the latter) is very perceptible. For our own individual self, we cannot see the reasons for such a change, nor are we aware of any causes which led to this step. That the imbibing of one gill[11] of spirits *per diem* by men who are exposed to all kinds of weather by day and by night—whose seasons of eating and sleeping are as changeable as the weather to which they are exposed—whose constitutions in one year may perhaps be forced to become acclimated to frigid regions and to torrid countries—that this, we say, is or has been the cause of any intemperance or any immorality in the navy, we cannot see, nor have we heard of. As a lover of temperance in drinking and eating we have always lauded the efforts of lecturers and moral suasionists; but being indifferent to total abstinence doctrines in either we have heretofore enjoyed the freedom of eating and drinking whatsoever we considered good for our health and comfort, and this freedom we have and always are willing to accord to all men. Therefore, not as an habitual rum-drinker or tippler, but as one who has a right to an opinion on any and every national question, we pronounce ourself to be opposed to this action of Congress. If the reform were really necessary, or if the allowance of spirituous liquors had an evil effect, either morally or physically, upon our seamen, we would hail it with pleasure for the good it would do to this mighty arm of our Government. That Congress will speedily see that it has committed a gross mistake in the passage of the act [eliminating the spirit ration], we have no doubt. The argument that the sailors "can do without it" is not sufficient cause for its total stoppage. Dangerous indeed would this argument become if carried further and applied either to our hard biscuit, our moldy pork or our allowance of unpalatable water.

————◦————

SEPTEMBER 3, 1862   This month was ushered in with quite a storm, the first day being one of drenching rain and high winds and the second and this being like unto it, although today it is more moderate. No doubt this was or is the equinoxial storm.[12] On the morning of the 1st we again dropped down the harbor to the navy yard, where we have since been anchored. The same evening the steamer *Ocean Queen* sailed for New Orleans with part of the troops who have been quartered in Pensacola for so long a time. As she passed out of that harbor she was saluted with twenty guns from Forts Pickens and Barrancas. The troops were under the command of Gen. [Lewis G.] Arnold, who previously commanded here. The command on his departure devolved on Col. [William "Billy"] Wilson.

Yesterday was a day of general rejoicing in the fleet, caused by the arrival of the mail steamer *Connecticut*. She brought a large mail and a supply of fresh beef, potatoes, onions, &c., showing us, as usual, that Uncle Sam does not entirely ignore the existence of his nephews in the Gulf.

Today nothing of any event has transpired, if we except the sailing of the *Jackson, Harriet Lane* and *Iroquois*.

Memorandum—We received three letters and four newspapers by the above mail and this morning occupied ourself in answering them.

————◦————

SEPTEMBER 12, 1862   Micawber-like, we have been "waiting for something to turn up"[13] since our last date in order to make a note of it; and even though several days have elapsed, we find on taking a retrospective view of things that there really is nothing of any import to chronicle. The expression "a dull monotony" would indicate well the occurrences of the six days next succeeding our last notes; and those of the latter were only variegated by leaving our anchorage at the navy-yard and coming up again to the city of Pensacola. When we add to this the fact of our lying there at present, that we wrote home on the 8th per bark *A. Houghton* (which, by the way, has not yet sailed) and that yesterday the steamer *Ocean Queen* brought and landed a considerable reinforcement from New Orleans, we have said all that can be said.

The weather is still warm, but it is kept comfortably so by occasional showers, and the nights are cool enough to sleep comfortably with a blanket. Fishing is still carried on to some extent by our crew, with varied success, sometimes every mess on board receiving a portion of the haul, which makes quite an addition to our rations.

———❦———

SEPTEMBER 17, 1862    After enduring an unabated storm of three days, we enjoyed this afternoon another view of the sun. Rains and high winds, when of but short duration even, may be spoken of as items or remarkable instances by those whom misfortune or necessity has exposed to their fury, and when the lengths of such extraordinary storms as the ones to which necessity has exposed us for the last few days is taken into consideration, we will be excused for making a note of it. Several complete drenchings during our frequent tours of sentry-go upon the hurricane deck of our steamer was all the accident that happened to us individually, and the majority, if not the entire crew, sustained the same damage. We must have been mistaken when we noticed the storm of the 1st and 2d inst. as the equinoxial storm: this, undoubtedly was the true one—at least, we hope it was, as another one of the kind, unless we are well housed, will not be acceptable.

Things present the same aspect as usual in the harbor, with no prospect of a change. We are lying at the navy-yard once more, where we have been for four days.

———❦———

SEPTEMBER 20, 1862    Today we are lying at Ship Island (Figure 80), where we arrived at half-past ten o'clock last night. The place, since our last visit, has undergone somewhat of a change. The sound of the drum is not so frequently heard on the barren sands and the white tent of the soldiery no longer cover its shores. Some, it is true, are still here,

FIGURE 80. Union Blockading Fleet off Ship Island—1862. From *Harper's Weekly*.

but the majority have left this place of drill and entered the practical school of war.

We left the navy-yard at Pensacola about 11 o'clock yesterday morning, in company with the *Jackson*. We had a beautiful day for sailing, and for our part we experienced much pleasure in the trip here. With the air sufficiently cool to make the rays of the sun agreeable, and with a clear bright sky above you and the gently swelling waters of the Gulf beneath, imparting such a pleasant, rolling motion to the vessel, one cannot help feeling happy, even though he be on an errand of rude war. Nothing of any note transpired on the way. We spoke the blockading fleet off Mobile about four o'clock in the afternoon.

The weather is still cool and pleasant, and the labor of coaling ship which we commence this afternoon, will be much lightened by cool breezes.

———◦———

SEPTEMBER 25, 1862   This beautiful morning finds us with a little leisure on our hands to devote to writing. We have before taken occasion to remark of pleasures experienced from viewing scenery which we have passed; and the enjoyment of such a day as this without remark is almost impossible. Since our last date, the weather has been a series of heavy gales and rain squalls, commencing in the afternoon of that

FIGURE 81. Fort Massachusetts on Ship Island—1862. From *Harper's Weekly*.

day and only dying away with the setting sun of yesterday. We were
then compelled to give over coaling ship and seek a secure anchorage
further in the sound, and today we go again alongside the coal-ship
to complete the job. The bright sun and the cool and almost bracing
weather we now enjoy makes ample amends for the wet weather of
the last few days.

We are still at Ship Island, about which we will further remark,
that a large casemated fort [Fort Massachusetts] is being about
erected on it (Figure 81).[14] Undoubtedly this spot may prove
a rendezvous for vessels trading along the Gulf coast and Lake
Pontchartrain, which will make such protection necessary; but if the
present news from the North in regard to the deficiency of the army
and its reverses be true, we think legislation might be used in more
useful channels, and means and money expended nearer home and
to more advantage for the good of the country. Eternal agitation and
legislation on a subject [slavery], the object of which had no deteriorating effect upon the country, produced a war. This is admitted on
all sides. Legislation, or too much of it, has crippled the movements
of the army in the North; this too, is apparent. Legislation in small
matters like rations has created murmurings and discontent in the
navy; and now the wasting of means and the employment of men
to populate a barren sand-bank far out of reach and almost out of

sight of [the] mainland, in perilous times like these, to say the least of it, shows very little of that wisdom which should emanate from Congress.

The *Ceres*, one of our river transport boats, arrived here yesterday from New Orleans, bringing [newspapers with] dates from there to the 21st. Everything was quiet in that city; but the information they had from the army of the Potomac was gloomy. The rebels were reported as everywhere victorious, and as having pushed into Maryland and threatening Pennsylvania with invasion.[15] We wait patiently for confirmation of this news, and only mention it as a warrant for our so closely scrutinizing the acts of our Government.

——◆——

**SEPTEMBER 29, 1862**   Since our last date we have made somewhat of a big move, and today we find ourselves anchored at a quite familiar place, viz: Pilot Town, at the southwest pass of the Mississippi river. Our first notes state that this place was a rendezvous for the fleet before the reduction of New Orleans, and from what we understand now it is used for the same purpose at present for a fleet to be used against Galveston, Texas, of which the *Westfield* is flag ship. The place has not altered any since we were last here, except that the low stage of the river has drained the surrounding land, and given a more comfortable aspect to the place. We notice also that the water of the river is quite clear, a circumstance that one would hardly have expected from the extreme muddiness of the past summer.

We started for this place on the 27th but the storm which was raging when we started increased to such an extent that we were compelled to put back. Yesterday, however, the weather cleared up, and at 8 o'clock in the evening we got under weigh once more, and after an extremely pleasant passage arrived here, via Pass a l'Outre, at half past nine this morning.

——◆——

**OCTOBER 1, 1862**   Today we commence another month, and that, too, while swiftly moving a few degrees farther South, thus seeming as if determined to keep the season of summer as long as possible. We have been under weigh since four o'clock yesterday afternoon, and have had remarkably fine weather so far. There is nothing for us to note, unless we apostrophize the vast expanse of water in which we are at present floating, and descant[16] upon the beautiful blue color which it presents; but we forbear. We have only opened our book to make a note of something we forgot on our last writing, viz: that we were in receipt of a letter from an old friend in Lancaster, on the 28th ult.

We will also stick the following "homily" in here, as being somewhat appropriate to an affair we noticed one month ago [when the spirit ration was stopped]:

## The Snake in the Glass—A Homily
BY JOHN G. SAXE[17]

Come listen to me, my lad;
Come listen to me for a spell;
Let that terrible drum
For a moment be dumb,
For your uncle is going to tell,
What befell
A youth who loved liquor too well.

A clever young lad was he, my lad;
And with beauty uncommonly blest,
Ere with brandy and wine,
He began to decline,
And behaved like a person possessed;
I protest,
The temperance plan is the best.

One evening he went to a tavern, my lad;
He went to a tavern one night,
And drinking too much
Rum, brandy and such;
The chap got exceedingly "tight;"
And was quite
What your aunt would entitle a "fright."

The fellow fell into a snooze, my lad;
'Tis a horrible slumber he takes;
He trembles with fear,
And acts very queer;
My eyes! How he shivers and shakes

When he wakes,
And raves about horrid great snakes!

'Tis a warning to you and to me, my lad;
A particular caution to all—
Though no one can see
The vipers but he—
To hear the poor lunatic bawl—
How they crawl—
All over the floor and the wall!

Next morning he took to his bed, my lad;
Next morning he took to his bed;
And he never got up
To dine or to sup,
Though properly physicked and bled,
And I read,
Next day, the poor fellow was dead.

You've heard of the snake in the grass, my lad;
Of the viper concealed in the grass;
But now you must know,
Man's deadliest foe
Is a snake of a different class
Alas!—
'Tis the viper that lurks in the glass!

A warning to you and to me, my lad;
A very imperative call:
Of liquor keep clear,
Don't drink even beer,
If you'd shun all occasion to fall,
If at all,
Pray take it uncommonly small.

And if you are partial to snakes, my lad;
(A passion I think rather low)
Don't enter to see 'em,
The Devil's Museum!—
'Tis very much better to go
(That's so!)
And visit a regular show.

# 8 The Capture of Galveston

OCTOBER 9, 1862 The last eight days have been fraught with events of a stirring character, in which the marines of the *Westfield* have taken a conspicuous part. On the 1st inst. we stated that we were under way for a more southern latitude, which we might have mentioned as being the city of Galveston, Texas;[1] and today we are lying off that place, having taken formal possession of it today by right of conquest. But we will note the intervening operations and movements which we have accomplished: On the night of the 1st inst. we came to anchor in the Gulf somewhere in the neighborhood of Sabine Pass,[2] where we lay until the next morning, when we sailed again for this harbor [Galveston], arriving the same evening. We lay outside, in company with the blockading fleet, until the 4th, for the purpose of reconnoitering and obtaining a pilot to take us through the intricate channel which leads to the city. On the morning of that day we sent a summons to the forts to surrender, which they refused to do; and in the afternoon we started in to drive them out. From all we could learn beforehand, we were led to expect quite a heavy fight; for such then we were prepared. Our squadron formed in line (Figure 82) in the following order, viz: *Westfield* (flagship), on the right, *Clifton*, with No. 19 bomb-schooner in tow, on the left, and the *Harriet Lane* and *Owasco* in the center. The fort [Fort Point] at the entrance of the harbor opened upon the *Westfield* at long range with a ten-inch columbiad, when we signaled to the rest of the vessels to open fire, which was responded to with eleven-inch shell and rifle shot from the center, and rifle shot from the left of the line; and with such effect that the Secesh made a regular skedaddle without taking time to reload their gun (Figure 83), which, by the way, proved to be the only one they

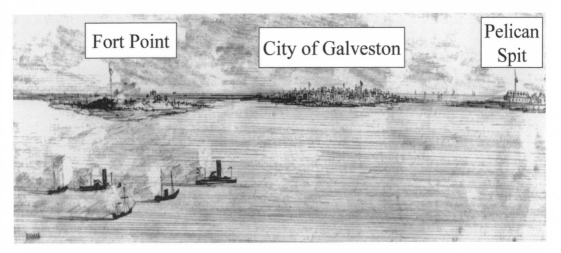

Fort Point | City of Galveston | Pelican Spit

FIGURE 82. The Capture of Galveston, Texas, October 1862. *Westfield* Entering Galveston Bay, Followed by *Owasco, Harriet Lane,* and *Clifton* Towing *Mortar 19.* Sketch No. 45 by Dr. Daniel D. T. Nestell. Identification Boxes Added by Editor. Courtesy of the Nestell Collection, Nimitz Library, U.S. Naval Academy, Annapolis, Maryland.

FIGURE 83. "Ye Defense of Ye City of Galveston, Texas: One Gun!" The Confederate Fort at Fort Point. Sketch No. 46 by Dr. Daniel D. T. Nestell. Courtesy of the Nestell Collection, Nimitz Library, U.S. Naval Academy, Annapolis, Maryland.

had.[3] In the meantime we proceeded up the harbor to engage other batteries which we understood to be there; but none were there except what were mounted with Quaker guns,[4] and so we turned our long rifle on the retreating rebels, considerably accelerating their before remarkable speed. When we came near the city, a battery of field pieces opened on us, but their shot fell short, and we quietly came to anchor in the harbor, notwithstanding their efforts to prevent us from doing so. A flag of truce was then sent off, demand-ing the surrender of the city and the raising of the stars and stripes within a certain time, accompanied with a threat to burn the place if not complied with;[5] and at the same time a party was sent ashore from the schooner to spike the battery [at Fort Point] which fired upon us. The next day a party was sent from the *Westfield* to another battery on the opposite side of the harbor [Pelican Spit], where the Secesh had also a commodious barracks. The guns upon this were found to be of the Quaker pattern, and one was brought off as a curiosity. It is quite a formidable looking thing, but being of wood of course is quite harmless. To complete the joke of fighting wooden guns, which had awed a large blockading fleet for a year, as well as to commemorate the occasion, we mounted it on the hurricane-deck, where it at least will be somewhat ornamental if not useful. In the afternoon the marines were ordered to go ashore and occupy the barracks aforesaid, and raise the American colors on the flagstaff. Both the getting ashore and the raising of the flag were matters of some difficulty, the former on account of the heavy sea running, and the latter because of the absence of halyards on the staff. But the marines were undaunted and after floundering through the surf for awhile soon gained the dry land with all their traps.[6] A little time also sufficed to rig the halyards, and at sunrise next morning the stars and stripes were proudly floating over our island. The marine guard of the *Clifton* landed soon after us, and regular barrack rules were soon in force and sentries posted. We anticipated a lengthy stay on "Pelican Spit,"[7] and therefore made ourselves as much at home as possible, but today we are longing for the cool breezes and surf bathing which our recall on board has deprived us of. These luxuries, together with the abundance of fish, game and oysters with which the island abounds, would have made a stay of six months quite acceptable. But as we have just intimated, we were recalled this morning for the purpose of accompanying the squadron up to the docks of the city. Soon after we came aboard we proceeded up, and this afternoon we were landed, in company with about one hundred sailors and the *Clifton*'s guard, for the purpose of raising the United States flag on the custom-house (Figure 84).[8] We found the wharves of the town guarded by the firemen in full uniform, by orders of the Mayor, and on landing they escorted us to the custom-house. The Mayor here received us, and expressed his pleasure at seeing the city once more about to pass into Union hands. He delivered the keys to Captain [Jonathan M.] Wainwright of the *Harriet Lane*,[9] who immediately took possession of the building and proceeded to the

FIGURE 84. Nineteenth-century Photograph of the U.S. Customhouse (1861) in Galveston, Texas. Courtesy of the Rosenberg Library, Galveston, Texas.

roof with a proper guard and raised the flag. The battalion presented arms as the colors were flung to the breeze, and the crowd of spectators expressed their delight in various patriotic remarks. Altogether it was quite a gala occasion for the marines and sailors and when we marched back to the boats nearly every one of our muskets was decorated with flowers, which the women and children gave to us. Of the people of Galveston we must say, that a more respectable and well behaved set we have never seen. Not a single sentry had to be detailed to keep the crowd back from the line. The modest distance kept by the ladies showed their good breeding, and the conduct of the numerous youngsters was a good example for the youth of our Northern cities.

OCTOBER 20, 1862 "Pelican Spit" is again occupied by the marines of the bomb flotilla. On Sunday, the 12th we were again ordered to go ashore, with one week's provision, much to our satisfaction. Our stay on board was signalized by being several times called to quarters for the purpose of dispersing some

FIGURE 85. Naval Gunners Firing a 100-pounder Parrott Rifle. From *Harper's Weekly*.

rebel cavalry who were bold enough to approach the city by way of the bridge from Virginia Point.[10] On all these occasions the immense distance and the extreme accuracy of the 100-pounder rifle gun of the *Westfield* (Figure 85) was proven with great satisfaction. Since we have been ashore, we have enjoyed ourselves, between the regular routine of barrack duty and picketing, in the various pastimes we have mentioned under our last date. The increasing warmth of the weather has, however, re-animated the mosquitoes and flies, the former of which make our nights somewhat uncomfortable. We long for a drenching rain and a cold spell to annihilate them. On Saturday last a mail steamer arrived from the North, in consequence of which a trip was made by us to the flagship for mails and provisions. Much to our disappointment there was nothing directed to our individual address.

———◦◦◦———

**OCTOBER 21, 1862**   The dangers and perils of picket duty have often been portrayed by correspondents for country newspapers during the present war, with such force, alloyed with such a vast amount of wordy patriotism, as to make the uninitiated believe there was a great deal of romance attached to it. The delusion which had overcome us among others on this subject was suddenly dispelled by a trial of it in the vicinity of Vicksburg. The repetition of it here [at Galveston], although accompanied by less apparent danger from the rebels, has in no wise altered our opinion of it. The mere fact of being posted far to the front of your companions for the purpose of keeping a bright lookout the livelong night may be of itself an easy task and on a clear moonlight night, somewhat romantic, especially if the picketer be a young man of susceptibility who has a "gal he left behind him."[11] But when one isn't very susceptible and don't happen to be in the other predicament just mentioned, and when the mosquitoes are as ravenous as they have been for the last few nights, we emphatically say picketing is a humbug. Even throughout the daytime these lively little insects keep tormenting us. The mosquitoes of the Mississippi are nowhere beside them, either in numbers or pertinacity. Confound 'em and confound the man who wouldn't get up in the middle of the night and burn his shirt to give light to curse them by. Again we say, oh, for a cold spell to annihilate the entire lot.

Yesterday afternoon we had another rowing match to the shipping, for the purpose of getting rations for a lot of contrabands [escaped slaves] who have been under our charge for the past week on the island. Blistered hands and somewhat stiffened limbs quite overbalanced the pleasure and healthful exercise we had anticipated. Pulling an oar in a ship's cutter in a heavy sea, for a couple of miles, is more like hard work than sport. We also had notice yesterday of an intended attack upon our island by the rebels, but after waiting patiently for them with everything in readiness for a warm reception we have begun to quit expecting them. Today, however, the flagship artillery has been booming at them from the upper end of the town; and we too have laid out the foundation of an earthwork for the purpose of making a stout resistance if they should be bold enough to venture across.

# 9 Matagorda Bay

"We know not what a day may bring forth,"[1] is a saw which every one has some opportunity of seeing verified. Today we are forcibly reminded of this. We had made up our minds, and also our preparations, for a lengthened stay upon the island [Galveston] where we last used our Note-Book, but this morning we find ourselves some one hundred miles from it. In the midst of a grand preparation for a somewhat

FIGURE 86. The *Clifton* "On the Breakers" Going Into Matagorda Bay. Sketch Shows Lighthouse on Matagorda Island in Center. Sketch No. 50 by Dr. Daniel D. T. Nestell. Courtesy of the Nestell Collection, Nimitz Library, U.S. Naval Academy, Annapolis, Maryland.

extensive oyster-bake, part of the marines (among whom was ourself) were recalled on board, and shortly after being ensconced there, we were under weigh for Matagorda Bay,[2] where we arrived at eight o'clock this morning (Figure 86), and are now lying for the purpose of sounding the channel in order to proceed safely up to a town situated at the head of the bay. In this case, also, we do not know what the next day, or even half-day, may bring forth nor will we anticipate. Our trip here was a delightful one, owing as well to its being somewhat a variety as to our leaving the numerous mosquitoes of the island behind us. This latter consideration, added to a fine cool breeze and the gentle rolling motion of the vessel, afforded us at least a rest for which we may be thankful.

---

OCTOBER 25, 1862    Matagorda Bay (Figure 87), we understand, is subdivided into three minor bays, consisting of Upper and Lower Matagorda and Lavaca bays.[3] The Lower Bay is the one in which we are this morning riding out a heavy gale, known in these latitudes as a "norther." Old sailors are expressing a thankfulness that we are not outside in the weather, and from the way the shallow water is here tossed about, we ourselves think we are far safer thus near to land than if far out in the Gulf, where the wind has full sweep at one and the water is of sufficient depth to admit of being thrown "mountain high." A decided change in the temperature is also apparent (54° Fahr. against 72° yesterday).

On the afternoon of the 23rd we started up the bay, but had not proceeded far before [we] missed the channel and ran hard aground.[4] Our consort, the *Clifton*, in endeavoring to aid us to get afloat again, got herself into the same predicament. We steamed and stormed with all our might for some hours, but all to no effect, and the fast ebbing tide left us only the tighter. We hoped the flowing tide would aid us to extricate ourselves, but we were disappointed, although the other vessel got afloat through its agency. Before the next flood tide we had lightened ourselves somewhat, by pumping the water from our tanks and at high water by a deal of steaming and a hearty pull from the *Clifton*, we were once more dragged into deep water, after being aground nearly twenty-four hours. In the meantime some of our officers had visited the adjacent shore, for the purpose of obtaining some fresh provisions, &c., and found the feelings of the inhabitants so thoroughly Secesh that they refused to sell a morsel of anything to a Union man.[5] Immensely patriotic, no

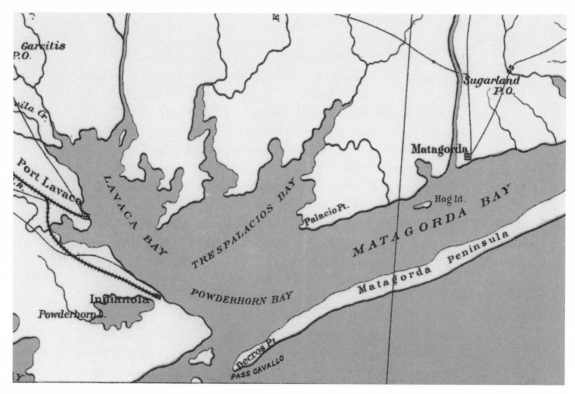

FIGURE 87. Map of Matagorda Bay Area, Texas. From the OR *Atlas*, Plate 157.

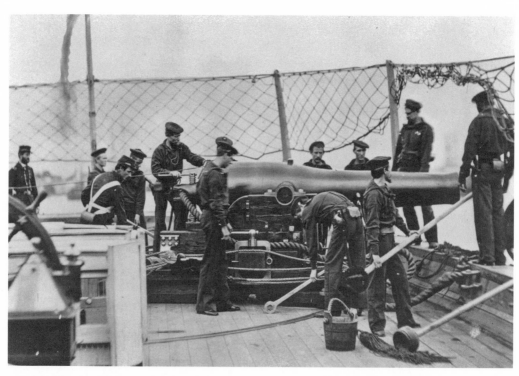

FIGURE 88. Matthew Brady Photograph of a 9-inch Dahlgren Gun Aboard an Unidentified U.S. Navy Warship During the Civil War. Courtesy of Navy Historical Center.

doubt, these Lone Stars thought this action was; very foolish indeed it would have proven if we had used the force at our hands and taken what we wanted gratis. Soon after we got under weigh again we descried[6] a sail ahead, to which we gave chase and soon overhauled. On firing a shot for her to heave to, her crew abandoned her and soon we discovered her to be on fire. This other patriotic Texan act was retaliated by our exploding a few 9-inch shell (Figure 88) over the escaping crew.[7] On boarding our prize, we found the fire had not gained much headway, and soon we had it extinguished. The schooner *Lecompte* is now astern with a prize crew aboard.[8]

OCTOBER 28, 1862 Today we are enjoying a fine day off the town of Matagorda.[9] The "norther" which we were enduring at our last writing has passed and weather mild as Spring has taken its place. On Sunday evening the thermometer was below 40°; today it ranges in the 60's. On Sunday morning [October 26] we raised our anchor and stood in for the town of "Powderhorn," or "New Indianola,"[10] (Figure 89) in sight of which we had anchored

FIGURE 89. "View of Indianola Taken from the Bay on the Royal Yard on Board the Barque *Texana*, Sept. 1860." Library of Congress.

to ride out the gale. A guard of marines, with an officer was sent ashore to bring off some of the "city fathers" for consultation with our Commodore.[11] They were accordingly brought; a lengthy confab was held in the cabin and we escorted them back. Whether the Union was safe in this vicinity or not we cannot positively say, but the fact of our visitors leaving in a very good humor, with sundry *Heralds* &c. in their hands,[12] and our weighing anchor soon after, leaves the inference that all was right in that quarter.[13] We heard here of sundry schooners having set sail when we first came in sight, and our hurry in leaving was also partly owing to the hope of capturing some or all of them as prizes. We had not gone far, however, when we discovered them (some 15 or 20) spread across the channel, their keels upon the bottom and their hulls beneath the water. Patriotism was high in Texas; most decidedly they do not love the Yankees as well as they professed they did in '46 [when Texas joined the United States]. Comment is useless—we leave the subject in disgust. The same evening we came to anchor where we are at present, some four miles from the town [of Matagorda], being unable to proceed farther for want of a sufficient depth of water.[14] Yesterday we employed our time in making boat expeditions to the town and an adjacent island [Hog Island], the result of which was the capture of 18 bales of cotton and the discovery of an immense oyster bed. The cotton was soon transferred aboard the *Westfield*, and the oyster bed underwent a good raking. The immense quantity of geese, ducks, &c., in the vicinity, also invited some of the ship's crew ashore for a day's sport. Oysters stewed, fried, roasted and on the shell were the order of the day, and today promises to be a repetition. Fresh beef is also obtainable and has been obtained. Regardless of Texan spleen we are also enjoying ourselves.

This morning a boat's crew from the *Clifton* captured a small cotton sloop. (We must reread the prize laws.)

———◦◦———

NOVEMBER 2, 1862    This, the first Sunday of the month, has been ushered in on board the *Westfield* with the usual monthly muster and inspection. We are still in the bay of Matagorda, although somewhat nearer the mouth than at our last writing. On the 29th ult. a mail steamer was reported in sight, and as the water would not admit of her coming up the bay to us we put down for her. (Mem.—letter and paper for us and several long overdue not yet arrived.) We returned the same evening, but

FIGURE 90. Bombardment of Port Lavaca, Texas (Spelled "Velaca" on Original Nestell Drawing), October 31 and November 1, 1862. Identification Boxes Added by Editor Replace Same Text Handwritten by Nestell. Sketch No. 49 by Dr. Daniel D. T. Nestell. Courtesy of the Nestell Collection, Nimitz Library, U.S. Naval Academy, Annapolis, Maryland.

instead of going to our old anchorage we turned off for the port of Lavaca,[15] situated on a different arm of the bay. The extreme shallowness and intricacy of the channel compelled us to lay to for the purpose of setting buoys to aid our return; and it was not until Friday, 31st, that we found ourselves able to demand the surrender of the town. This being refused,[16] we in the afternoon made an attack (Figure 90) upon the defenses of the town, consisting of some four batteries and mounting in all some eight or ten guns. They returned the fire quite vigorously with round and rifle shot, showing us both good guns and good gunnery.[17] We kept up the fight until sundown, but owing to the nature of the channel could not come to close quarters with them. At this moment our 100-pounder Parrott gun bursted (Figure 91),[18] wounding three men and depriving us of our most effective long range weapon. We retired out of range of the batteries and anchored for the night. Lucky as has been the career of the *Westfield* the bursting of this gun was the crowning streak. Never before has such an accident to such a piece of ordnance been attended with so little damage.[19]

Yesterday morning we renewed the bombardment, but running short of ammunition for our remaining guns, we retired after two hours and a half's firing,[20] and today we are lying just inside of the bar, feeling somewhat "down in the mouth." To add to our misfortunes, we were notified at muster this morning that provisions were short, and therefore our allowance must be curtailed for the present.

FIGURE 91. Bursting of the 100-pounder Gun on Board the Steamer *Juniata*, 1864. From *Harper's Weekly*.

NOVEMBER 6, 1862 We left Matagorda Bay on the after noon of Tuesday (4th) and arrived at Galveston early the next morning, at which place we are now lying. Another of these "northers" for which these latitudes are noted is raging, but with our usual luck the *Westfield* was safely anchored before it commenced.

On our way here we overhauled and spoke the ship *Morning Light* of the blockading squadron. On arriving in sight of the harbor [at Galveston] we found the gunboat *Owasco* (aground on the bar).[21] This accident gave us an appetizing job before breakfast, but we had the satisfaction of getting her afloat in a very short time.

Affairs are about the same as when we left here—the town is quiet, the vessels off the town ditto, and Pelican Island is still occupied by the Marines. We understand, however, that the *Owasco* has been up to Virginia Point on a reconnaissance and exchanged shots there with the rebels. We hear too that a rebel ram has been discovered at the head of the bay. This latter, however, we consider doubtful.

# 10 The Battle of Galveston

NOVEMBER 12, 1862 Galveston, Texas is yet our stopping place. Since our last arrival here we have been spending the time around in the various ways for which seamen are so noted—spinning yarns, twisting ropes, sewing, sleeping and (we were going to say chewing tobacco, but we bethink ourself that we have been out of the weed for some weeks, and the latter, therefore, is not a general but an occasional pastime). We begin to think that we have rather many mistakes of our redoubtable Uncle [Sam] to note this while past. The wisdom of the act of July 12 [stopping the spirit ration] might have been forgotten if it had not been so closely followed by the existing state of affairs; it must be a culpable neglect that leaves us on our coasts without provisions and without small stores. But we forbear.

This morning we started outside for the purpose of taking in coal from the coal ship, but the heavy swell of the sea prevented us from going alongside and so we returned to our anchorage. On the way up we took our prize, the *Lecompte*, in tow, which had arrived from Matagorda the night before. A heavy rain (the first we have had on the coast of Texas) is now keeping us between decks.

---

NOVEMBER 16, 1862 Were we writing a novel instead of a log-book we could start this chapter with quite a summary of contents. Our small capitals and dashes would run thus: The alarm—Surprise—Recall of the Marines—Distinguished Visitor—Speech of the Commodore—Deserters—&c. But our object is to give the contents without a summary attached. Under date of the 6th we noticed a rumor, of which we expressed a doubt, that a rebel ram had made its appear-

FIGURE 92. Commander William B. Renshaw, Captain of U.S.S. *Westfield*. From the Massachusetts Commandery, Military Order of the Loyal Legion Collection. U.S. Army Military History Institute, Carlisle, Pennsylvania.

ance near Pelican Spit. Since then we have been convinced of the truth of the rumor by the removal of the *Owasco* to the Spit and by talking to those who really saw her. A rumor of a meditated attack by some rebel steamers upon our fleet has also been rife for more than a week. At first the rumor was laughed at, but from information we have received from persons on shore, it now seems probable that such an attack may be made. On Friday last we were all called to muster for the purpose of receiving this information, and of being warned, if possible, to keep a more vigilant lookout when on duty. Our Captain (Figure 92) made us quite a neat little speech—curt, pithy and patriotic; like everything else he has done since he has been our commander, it was for our own good, and we all received it as such.

"My lads," said he, "I have called you together to tell you that there is a rumor afloat that an attempt will be made some of these nights to drive us from the harbor, by some rebel steamers, and I have reason to believe there is some truth in the rumor. Now what I want to impress on you is that you must keep your eyes wide open, to prevent a surprise; be ready at your guns at the first alarm. I know I have a good crew—I couldn't wish a better set of men; but here in an enemy's country I can't impress it upon your minds too strongly to be vigilant. If we are attacked at all it will be by boats drawing very little water, and they may come upon us without coming though the channel; and their object will be to board us. So you must keep your eyes all around you; for if they get alongside before we are ready to receive them, or before our anchor is up, they may stand a pretty good job of succeeding; but if we are under weigh, I know—with the good stout engine of the *Westfield* and her gallant crew—we can sink and destroy a good half-dozen of them. I am fully determined not to be driven from here, and I know you will stand by me to the last to prevent such a thing. I have not the least doubt of your bravery; I have had sufficient proofs of that, but what I want to impress upon you is to be, if possible, more vigilant. As I said before, if they catch us napping they may succeed, but if we are wide awake when they come, I'll be d——d if they will."

Early the same morning (14th) a boat's crew from the *Owasco*, who had gone over to the main land on a foraging expedition, were fired upon by a party of rebels in ambush, and nearly the whole of them wounded. Two of them were left for dead, but managed to crawl to the beach and were taken aboard again, and the rest were carried off as prisoners.[1] This was more proof that the rebels were close upon us, and in the afternoon the *Owasco* was ordered to anchor among the fleet and the marines from Pelican Spit were brought on board. Three deserters also came on board the same day from Clear Creek, about forty miles from here. They came the whole way by water notwithstanding the vigilance of the rebels. They report the conditions of things in Secessia [the South] as very deplorable, and say that there is much Union sentiment in Texas. They were men of Northern birth, who had been impressed into the rebel service, and this was the first opportunity they had of leaving it. There are many more of the same kind waiting for a chance to desert, they say.[2]

On Saturday morning a British war steamer was reported at anchor outside the bar, and many speculations were made as to her particular business here at present. Before noon her gig was alongside the *Westfield*, and her captain in the cabin. She proved to be H.B.M. [Her British Majesty's] sloop-of-war *Greyhound*, but her mission nor the name of her Captain has not yet transpired. Our prize, the *Lecompte*, was tendered to him for the purpose of returning to his vessel, and he went aboard early in the afternoon. Our Yankee sailors had a very poor chance to display their seamanship before him, against a narrow channel, a strong headwind and a flowing tide. They beat out, however, till near the bar, when they were becalmed; and night coming on they returned on board. We are at this moment (2 o'clock P.M.) preparing to give him a steamboat ride to his vessel, as the weather has cleared up and we are going out to the coal-ship. Half an hour ago the *Clifton* returned from New Orleans. She brought a mail which had been lying there for us. Among it was something for ourself, but it was quite ancient.

---

**NOVEMBER 20, 1862**    We attempted, as noticed under our last date, to carry our "distinguished visitor," the British Captain, to his vessel, but after coming down to the bar we found the water too rough to admit of our passing outside, and accordingly we returned with him on board. The next morning we made another attempt, and this time were successful. Sir [Henry D.] Hickley, notwithstanding the roughness of the sea, was soon on board the *Greyhound*,³ and she soon after [was] under weigh for the Mexican coast. We occupied ourself the balance of the day in coaling ship, being compelled to transport it in bags by boats from the coal-ship to the *Westfield*. We returned in the evening and lay at our old anchorage, without anything of note transpiring, until last evening, when we dropped down to Bolivar channel on the other side of Pelican Spit, to intercept some vessels which we had heard would attempt to get to sea by this route in the night. None attempted it, however, and we are this morning still at anchor off the Spit, with a strong gale blowing and the weather extremely cold. We should mention that on Tuesday night last we had a false alarm sounded, to see how quick we could be brought to quarters. In three and a half minutes we were ready for action.

---

**NOVEMBER 23, 1862**    Sunday has dawned upon us clear and warm, and the soft spring-like weather of today is quite a contrast to the blustering winds we noticed under our last date. Then we noted that no vessels had attempted to run out through the channel we were blockading, but it seems we stated things prematurely. Shortly after closing our book, a sloop was observed ashore across the peninsula where we were lying. The two cutters were immediately manned and sent to her.

On approaching her, the crew deserted her and set her on fire. A hearty pull, however, brought our boys alongside in time to save everything on board except her papers. She was soon lightened and got afloat, and with three cheers from the new crew she was soon sailing astern of the *Westfield*. She was heavily laden with cotton, containing over sixty bales. She sails for New Orleans today to be sold. Last Wednesday the *Lecompte* was also sent there for the same purpose. Our old companion, the *Sachem*, came in on Thursday evening from Corpus Christi, short of provisions. She was supplied and left again on Saturday morning. The *Fairy*—a fairy-like man of war—came from Sabine Pass on the same errand, and left again the same day supplied. The barque *Arthur* arrived outside today with mail &c. from Pensacola via the *Rhode Island*.

---

NOVEMBER 26, 1862   Today, though a date of no particular note in history, is one of importance to ourself, being no less than the anniversary of our birth. That event is recorded in the Family Bible at home as having occurred on the 26th day of November, A.D. 1837—making us, therefore, today exactly 25 years of age. It is natural for one to look back and review his past life on days like this. He is forcibly reminded that he is progressing onward in years, and though long and tedious have seemed the days and months as they were passing by, yet when we bethink ourselves of the occurrences [since] our last natal anniversary, and even the one prior to that, we are struck by the swiftness with which years are accumulating upon us. Two years ago we spent this day in the pursuits of peace at home and the number of our years was unheeded. The next found our beloved country torn by treason and divided by civil war, and ourself in the ranks of the defenders of the constitution and the laws. Today we are helping to represent that constitution and to uphold it in one of the traitor-States. Where the next shall find us we know not. But we dismiss the subject, leaving hopes for the future unexpressed, and accepting our fate as a soldier and a bachelor with all the grace in our power.

Since our last date we have again coaled ship. And have experienced another of those "northers." The latter has driven us ashore on Pelican Spit, and we are not yet afloat.

---

**NOVEMBER 28, 1862**    We got the old *Westfield* afloat again all safe and sound, the same evening, and took up our anchorage again in the Bolivar channel,[4] where we are now lying. Yesterday, being the day which the Governors of the different States usually set apart as a day of Thanksgiving,[5] was kept as a sort of holiday by our crew. The ship was gaudily dressed with ensigns and signals of different colors, and no unnecessary work required of the men. The roast turkey, pumpkin pie and doughnuts, so prevalent and indispensable around home in the celebration of that day, were easily dispensed with by us, and for most urgent reasons. Perhaps, however, our thanks were just as hearty upon a fill of biscuit and pork as they would have been upon more sumptuous fare.

Nothing of any moment has transpired in the last few days, and nothing, therefore, can be commented on. Even the weather refuses to make any sudden changes, and its pleasantness is too well adapted to our own temperament to admit of us filling up a page on that subject in the way of grumbling. Add to this the fact that we are again on full rations and have plenty of tobacco, and we may say that we are as near perfectly happy as a marine can be.

---

**NOVEMBER 30, 1862**    Yesterday was quite a day of excitement for our crew. We were just finishing up a thorough holystoning[6] of the decks and general clearing up of the vessel, fore and aft, when the lookout reported a rebel ram coming down the bay. Soon we could all make out a low black object moving with considerable rapidity toward us. We hurried our work through and cleared the decks for action, expecting for a certainty that she would offer us battle, seeing that we were alone in the channel, and too far from our other vessels to hope for assistance from them. On she came, until her dirty rebel flag could be easily distinguished, when we thought it time to up anchor and meet her half way. But, lo! She saw our move in an instant, and turning round with an astonishing swiftness, she steamed up the bay as if the devil had kicked her, with the *Westfield* in full chase. We gained rapidly on her, but our paddlewheels beginning to stir up the mud rather extensively, warned us that if we followed much farther we would be aground. Accordingly, we gave up the chase, first sending a 9-inch shell after her, which fell short. Today there are no signs of her, and everything is quiet. The *Lecompte* returned from New Orleans this morning.

DECEMBER 2, 1862    The newly initiated month has brought with it a high wind and drizzling rain, making everything damp and uncomfortable on deck. A wet day on shore, where amusements are plenty and society varied, is a bore, and has been written so by many who have made human nature their study; but to be cooped up in the small space allotted to "hands" on board a war vessel, is a misery in damp weather. Everybody is too wet to talk in a good humor, and so they growl; everything is too damp to admit of a snooze, and that causes everyone to grumble; and so the hours drag along, each seeming in itself a watch, and the day itself seems like an age. But bad and good go hand in hand on board a man-of-war as at other places, and so we accept it.

Last evening we were somewhat startled by our ships at the town [Galveston] opening a heavy fire, and this morning we came over to see what was the matter. It seems that the Union inhabitants, who have taken up their abode on one of the lower wharves of the town, under the guns of the shipping, were attacked by a party of rebels from the Point, who also fired upon the shipping. They were soon dispersed, with some of their number killed and wounded.[7]

DECEMBER 4, 1862    Last night was again made somewhat exciting by the firing of heavy guns and a small pyrotechnic display, but rebeldom had nothing to do with it. The steamer *Tennessee*[8] arrived outside this harbor, and made known her arrival by the above means. She brought a supply of provisions for the Galveston fleet and a small mail from New Orleans, but no late news. Yesterday a foraging party from our vessel landed on Bolivar Point for the purpose of procuring some fresh meat from among the numerous cattle roaming around there. The fate of the *Owasco*'s foraging party at the same place some weeks ago made us cautious enough to fire an 8-inch shell into the bushes before landing. Whether this kept the rebels from attacking us or not, of course, cannot be told—at least they did not molest us; but it appeared to fill the cattle with great fear, for no sooner did we approach them than a general stampede took place. One cow was too slow, however, and was soon turned into beef. The way the meat persisted in holding together today at dinner tells why this animal was more unfortunate than her fellows. Texas cattle, when young, are as fleet of foot as Texas soldiers.

———◦—◦——

**DECEMBER 7, 1862**   Rumors of attacks to be made upon us by the rebels from Virginia Point are as plenty as fiddlers in the lower regions, every night bringing a fresh one from the Union inhabitants on shore.[9] Although such things do not frighten us badly, they do have the effect of keeping us more watchful. Today we received a visit from three of the Secesh officers from the Point under a flag of truce, but what their object was has not yet become known to the men. They left in a very good humor— so we have recorded of the visitors we entertained at Powderhorn. We thought then the "Union was safe" there, but found out a day or two afterwards [at Lavaca] it was not. We will not venture an opinion here lest we be again mistaken. Yesterday we received information from Sabine Pass that several steamers and a ram were meditating an attack upon our blockading vessels there.[10] The *Clifton* was sent around to reinforce them. The weather has again approached the beautiful, and everybody is glad of it again. The change took place yesterday morning, but whether the eclipse of the moon, which took place on Friday night, had anything to do with it, we cannot say, our knowledge of astronomy not being extended enough to make us positive on that point.

———◦—◦——

**DECEMBER 11, 1862**   Still at Galveston and everything quiet, notwithstanding the continued rumors of our being attacked and driven from here. The *Clifton* returned from Sabine Pass on Sunday night and reported everything right there. On Monday morning she went up near the bridge which connects Galveston Island with [Virginia] Point, where the rebels appeared to be building a battery,[11] and fired a few shell[s]. A skedaddle among the Secesh was the consequence of this move, and they have kept clear of the place ever since. Yesterday was somewhat of a busy day aboard in the way of pulling and hauling. We stowed our old 100-pounder out of the way and took on board another 9-inch Dahlgren[12] from the *Clifton*. The old coal barge we have had occasion to mention so often, was of great service to us on this occasion, her foreyard making an excellent shears for the purpose. The

*Westfield* may be said to be in complete fighting trim again, although not quite so effective as when she first went into commission. But what we lack in metal, perhaps we can make up in the long experience we have had in handling great guns. The *Tennessee* left a few days ago for New Orleans.

———◦——◦———

**DECEMBER 14, 1862**    A quiet but somewhat cloudy Sabbath is ending another week of monotony. Nothing of any importance has transpired, and there seems to be a decided lull in the storm of war. Early last week the inhabitants of Galveston were notified by means of hand-bills posted throughout the town, that after Thursday evening all communication between the town and Virginia Point would be cut off, and a chance offered to all who wished to leave to do so. The Union inhabitants on the lower wharves took various meanings out of this notice, and became more clamorous for protection from the Commodore, who offered all who wished it a passage to New Orleans.[13] The coal bark *Island City*, being now empty, was accordingly chartered for this purpose, and on Friday some hundred or so went on board.[14] As a precautionary measure, the *Harriet Lane* and *Owasco* were moved further above the town to have a better view of the movements of the rebels and prevent them from coming down so close. The desertion of the town by the Union-men also made us dubious about the fort below the town [Fort Point] and the gun still there.[15] An attempt was made by our gunners yesterday to burst the gun, but was unsuccessful. It was however rendered useless and the magazine burned.

———◦——◦———

**DECEMBER 19, 1862**    Today is Friday—the Friday before Christmas, and the last but one of the year 1862; and although scarce noon, an item is produced for our noting. One of the bomb-schooners (the *Rachel Seaman*) arrived this morning from the blockade off some of the Texas ports, her business (unknown); news, none. Yesterday a steamer and two barks hove in sight, and for a while caused quite a sensation among us, we supposing that the long-expected mail steamer from the North and the troops promised for here were now surely come. But both these suppositions proved erroneous, as a nearer approach to them proved the steamer to be the *Tennessee*, from New Orleans, with a new rifle and a small mail for us, and the barks the *Cavallo* and *Elias Pike*, from the same place with coal. We have not yet taken the new gun aboard, the weather being too rough to admit of our laying alongside the steamer.

On Wednesday we were practiced at target firing with the great guns at 1350 yards, and with small arms at 50 yards. The shooting was pronounced good by the Commodore.

———— ◦●◦ ————

**DECEMBER 21, 1862**    We finished up Friday by running along side the dock at Pelican Spit, for the purpose of hoisting our old and now useless rifle out to make room for the new one. Early on Saturday the derrick was rigged, and before noon "Old Tom" was laid upon the dock; although on account of the shears giving way, he came very nigh being laid at the bottom of the channel. In the afternoon we were all allowed to run ashore, and soon the island was covered with yelling sailors and very noisy marines. "Leap frog," "shindy,"[16] wrestling and racing were indulged in in a manner which would have made schoolboys' mouths water to have participated in. "Go it while you're young," the reckless youth exclaim;[17] and "Go it when you get a chance," should be the motto of sober men—and especially seamen. Men are but overgrown boys when let loose from the discipline of a man-of-war upon a beautiful island. Today we were again allowed ashore, but were recalled about 3 o'clock for the purpose of towing the *Rachel Seaman* out, she lying along near the dock, taking in water.[18] We are again in Bolivar Channel.

———— ◦●◦ ————

**DECEMBER 26, 1862**    Christmas is over—gone—past; nor was it in any respect dissimilar to other days. Even the quiet of Sunday was not ours; and the same ration which a common day would have brought, we thankfully received. Well, its novelty may after all be of some benefit; and at some future Christmas, if we are spared to spend another in civil life, the remembrance of this and the last one may add a greater zest to the roast fowl, pies, puddings and bonbons in which we may then be indulging. We hope so. On the 24th the steamer *Saxon* arrived from New Orleans with part of the troops for here, and yesterday morning they were landed under the guns of the fleet. They numbered some

400 and were part of the 42nd Massachusetts.[19] At the time of the steamer's arrival two rebel officers were aboard us under a flag of truce. They left after she had come to anchor within a cable's length of us. One of the coal barks has been towed inside and is now unloading at Pelican Spit. The weather is exceedingly fine, and the gentle breezes which we are enjoying might with truth be called zephyrs. The rebels at [Virginia] Point have daily practice with their guns, and, judging from their sound, they have some whappers up there.

---

**DECEMBER 28, 1862**    The rifle gun is on board at last and the *Westfield* is "herself again." The gun itself may be a good one, but the bursting of our last, we must confess, has made us somewhat dubious of Parrotts, and this has much the shape of a Parrott, and, in our judgment, is not so good as the genuine. To be brief, it is nothing but an old "long 32" rifled and bound at the breech with wrought iron. We went outside yesterday to the *Tennessee* for the purpose of taking it aboard, but we only succeeded in swinging it from the steamer to the bark *Cavallo*, when darkness put an end to our work. We intended to tow the bark inside and shift the gun at our leisure, but from some rumpus kicked up between the skipper and the Commodore, we went inside without her. This morning, however, things appeared to have cooled down, and we proceeded out again, took the gun aboard and towed the bark inside. This and the taking of ammunition aboard made an unusual Sabbath for us, and, as on rainy Sundays, divine service was dispensed with. The *Tennessee* has left for New Orleans again. The weather is still very fine, and everything is quiet in town.

---

**DECEMBER 30, 1862**    There has been considerable excitement here since our last date. Yesterday morning we had three arrivals, but no news. The gunboat *Sachem*, from Corpus Christi, was the principal one of these. The other two were the *Lecompte*, from Matagorda, and a man-of-war schooner from down the coast—quite a Lilliputian, by the way, but carrying a battery of two rifle guns. With these vessels also came a heavy rain, which lasted throughout the entire day and part of last night, when the wind shifted to the north, and we are now experiencing another of those cold "northers" we have so often before mentioned. About

2 o'clock, just as the "norther" had commenced, we were somewhat startled by the lighthouse on Bolivar Point, within gunshot of us, taking fire. It, together with the keeper's dwelling, burned brightly until daylight, and this morning a heap of ruins occupies the place of this handsome and useful structure.[20] This vandalism is characteristic of the rebels, and was undoubtedly the work of Texan guerillas. Government property appears to be poor stock, even when covered by the muzzles of government cannon. Everything is quiet in town, these *bold* guerillas not daring to attack the few hundred Yankees there.

---

## JANUARY 10, 1863

A great change has taken place in the aspect of affairs since our last noting. Then we were on the *Westfield*; now we are on the *Clifton* (Figure 93). Then, too, we were at Galveston; now we are on our way thither. Our New Year was ushered in with the roar of artillery and the din of battle (Figure 94).[21] At midnight all was quiet and serene; at daylight the *Harriet Lane* was in the hands of the rebels (Figure 95), the *Westfield* was aground, and everything in confusion; at 10 o'clock

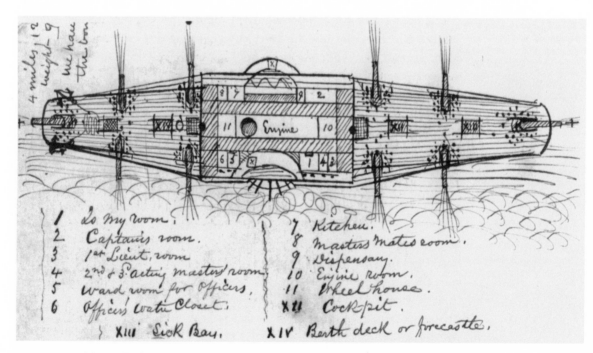

FIGURE 93. The Deck of U.S.S. *Clifton* in Fighting Order. Sketch No. 75 by Dr. Daniel D. T. Nestell. Courtesy of the Nestell Collection, Nimitz Library, U.S. Naval Academy, Annapolis, Maryland.

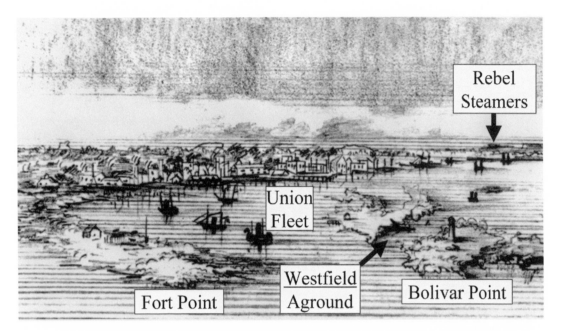

FIGURE 94. The Recapture of Galveston, Texas, January 1, 1863. Sketch No. 52 by Dr. Daniel D. T. Nestell. Identification Boxes Added by Editor Replace Same Text Handwritten by Nestell. Courtesy of the Nestell Collection, Nimitz Library, U.S. Naval Academy, Annapolis, Maryland.

FIGURE 95. Capture of U.S.S. *Harriet Lane* at Galveston, Texas, January 1, 1863. Sketch No. 51 by Dr. Daniel D. T. Nestell. Courtesy of the Nestell Collection, Nimitz Library, U.S. Naval Academy, Annapolis, Maryland.

FIGURE 96. "Attack of the Rebels Upon Our Gun-Boat Flotilla at Galveston, Texas, January 1, 1863." Destruction of the *Westfield* (Center Right). From *Harper's Weekly*.

the *Westfield* was blown up (Figure 96), and with her Commodore [William B.] Renshaw, Lieutenant [Charles W.] Zimmerman, Engineer [W. R.] Green, Gunner's Mate [John] Callahan, Quarter-gunner [Sam P.] King, Coxswain [W. Easer] Esser; Seamen—[Henry] Bothke, [Rodolphus C.] Hibbard, [Peter] Johnson and [Mathew] McDonald; Firemen—[George E.] Cox, [William] Reeves and [Hugh] McCabe; and the rest of the crew were on their way to New Orleans in the transports *M.A. Boardman* and *Saxon*. It was a disgraceful defeat. We arrived at New Orleans on Sunday, 4th and remained until the 9th for repairs, &c., to some of the vessels, when the *Clifton* started back, with ourself and some six or eight more of the *Westfield's* crew added to her.[22] Received four letters and half a dozen papers while at New Orleans and wrote home.

# 11 The Capture of U.S.S. Hatteras

**JANUARY 21, 1863** This keeping a Note-Book is getting to be a bore. Aboard the old craft [*Westfield*] we had some little conveniences for writing, which made it a pleasure to write a few notes; but here [on *Clifton*] we have nothing—even the ink we have thus far used requiring a large amount of "cheek" to borrow. Perhaps when we are better acquainted things may go better; if not, we will dispense with writing altogether.

Since our last, much has taken place. We left ourselves on the road to Galveston. We arrived there the same evening, and it being dark when we came upon the fleet lying there, we had some difficulty in making them believe we were really a "Simon pure"[1] Yankee craft. We soon settled the question, however, to their satisfaction, notwithstanding their suspicions having caused them to beat to quarters and train their guns on us, and for the rest of the night we lay quietly at anchor. Sunday broke calm and beautiful upon us, and preparations were made for an attack upon the town early next morning. The vessels we found there were the sloop-of-war *Brooklyn*, and the gunboats *Sciota*, *Cayuga*, *New London* and *Hatteras*. In the afternoon a strange craft hove in sight, and the *Hatteras* went in chase.[2] Just after dark heavy firing was heard in the direction the *Hatteras* had taken, about twelve miles distant, which caused the entire fleet to get under way. The *Brooklyn* and *Sciota* put to sea and the rest of us came to anchor again further out. The two mentioned vessels not returning again that night, the attack on the city was postponed. They returned about noon on Monday, 12th, but could gain no information as to the firing. The same evening the gig of the *Hatteras* came in, and the crew reported that about dark they came up with the strange sail, and upon hailing received answer that it was H.B.M. sloop *Spitfire*. The *Hatteras*

FIGURE 97. United States Troops Raise the Flag Over the State Capitol in Baton Rouge, Louisiana. From *The Soldier in Our Civil War*, vol. 2.

then lowered a boat to go on board, when the stranger opened her broadside upon her, which the *Hatteras* returned. A running fight then took place, and after the firing had ceased the *Hatteras* could not be found, and the boat steered for the fleet. The same evening the rest of the *Hatteras*'s boats were picked up, from which it is inferred that she was sunk and all hands perished. The stranger is supposed to have been the notorious "290."[3] The *Clifton* was immediately sent to New Orleans with dispatches, where, after a rough passage, we arrived on the 16th. We took in coal on the 17th, with the intention of returning next day, but upon representation being made to the Admiral that the boat was unseaworthy he ordered us up the [Mississippi] river,[4] and on Sunday the 18th, we found ourselves at Baton Rouge (Figure 97). On our way up we stopped at Plaquemine, and dispatched the *Katahdin* to New Orleans, which looks very much as if we were to exchange places with her on the Galveston line, and which would be no more than right, as she was built with the intention of being a sea-boat and the *Clifton* with the view of plying smooth water. Baton Rouge is again occupied by the Union soldiers protected by the sloop-of-war *Richmond* and the ram *Essex*.[5] We laid there until the evening of the 14th, when we dropped down again to Plaquemine, where we are still lying, watching the town and covering the Union troops along the banks of the river. The gunboat *Albatross* is also here. The *Kineo* was also here, but went down the river yesterday. The weather is clear and cold—much colder than we expected to find any weather in "Dixie." Frosts equal to any seen in Pennsylvania are to be seen every morning, and ice forms quite as fast as there. Some contrabands came on board during last night.

# 12 *A New Commander*

**FEBRUARY 9, 1863**    Today we are lying at a somewhat familiar spot—no less a place than Ship Island. Things have about the same aspect as our former sojourn here. The fort we mentioned [Fort Massachusetts], and condemned, as being built here, is nearly finished now, and our opinion of its usefulness is somewhat altered. The Emancipation Proclamation appears to be playing the devil here also. N[egroes] are now garrisoning the island and all the white soldiers are under arrest for refusing to recognize them. Big thing![1] From our last date until Feb. 5th, we were in the Mississippi; sometimes at Plaquemine and sometimes at Baton Rouge. On the latter date we were ordered down the river to New Orleans, and from there here, with all dispatch. We arrived here on the evening of the 7th, and found affairs somewhat excited. Rams and rumors of rams were all the go, and our arrival was hailed with joy by the fleet and the moaks.[2] We found here the *Jackson*, the *Vincennes*[3] and the *Relief*. Last night a suspicious light, moving in the Sound in the direction of Mobile, caused an alarm in the fleet and on shore. We may yet have some fun with rebel rams.[4]

**FEBRUARY 17, 1863**    Since our last writing, nothing of importance has transpired. We left our anchorage the day before yesterday, and took a cruise around the Sound, stopping awhile at the "back entrance" to Mobile; but we returned the same evening.

The U.S. transport *Union* was here about a week ago, bringing a mail and some fresh "grub" for us; good humor and high living has been the go ever since, but both are now on the decline. The news from the North, like everything we have heard this year, was far from cheering. Of four expeditions (against Vicksburg, Richmond, Kinston and Murfreesboro) but one was successful, and that success was dearly bought. Legislation on N[egroes] and Generals is not doing the cause much good. We had an idea when we enlisted that the war was for the preservation of the Union and that McClellan was our most able General; now we have an idea that the war is for the abolition of slavery and that [William S.] Rosecrans[5] is a better General than Burnside, McClellan, and Pope, combined. Strange how circumstances will alter opinions! Therefore we make a note of it.

---

**FEBRUARY 22, 1863**  Washington's birthday! A day of joy and thankfulness to all who revere him as the "Father of his Country." But what a contrast! He left us a country prosperous, peaceful, and respected by all nations; and today we are torn by discord and civil war, our manufactures and commerce at a stand still, and we the laughingstock of the world! May the next anniversary see us once more united in peace and harmony, and treason forever crushed. Notwithstanding war time, the day has been duly celebrated at Ship Island. The ship-

FIGURE 98. United States Steamer Firing on a Confederate Steamer Near Ship Island. From *Frank Leslie's Illustrated Famous Leaders and Battle Scenes of the Civil War.*

ping [ships in the fleet] are gaily decorated with flags and banners, and at noon each fired a salute of 21 guns. The fort on the island also fired a salute.[6] A boat regatta also came off in honor of the day, yesterday afternoon, today being Sunday. In the regatta our cutters came in third, the *Jackson*'s two boats beating her by about 50 yards. This morning we had some excitement in chasing a supposed rebel steamer (Figure 98), but after bringing her to, she proved to be the *General Banks*, one of the Union transports. On Friday we were up the Sound again, and returned same day.

———— ✦ ————

**FEBRUARY 24, 1863**    Today we are lying off Fort Morgan, Mobile Bay, having come here with dispatches to the Commodore of the blockading fleet. The frigate *Susquehanna* and four gunboats are here. News about here is as scarce as at Ship Island. We finished up Washington's birthday by paying a visit to the *Jackson*, to see some old friends, and upon our return, our vessel proceeded up the Sound on a reconnaissance, returning the same night. Yesterday morning we again went up, and on the way picked up five deserters from rebeldom—two from their army and three from their navy. Of course they gave dismal accounts of the situation of the rebels in Mississippi, and of course we believed them. At least their tales were cheering, and their news of importance enough to take us to Mobile Bay. On our way back to Ship Island we passed some dozen enormous flocks of wild duck, and all hands were given the privilege of firing at them. The weather is beginning to get extremely summer-like, so much so that we have discarded underclothing as superfluous.

———— ✦ ————

**FEBRUARY 26, 1863**    "Music hath charms," &c.[7]—we were going to add under our last date, to continue the recital of the pleasures we were enjoying aboard, beside duck-shooting; but unfortunately we capsized our ink, and instead of spending another hour in writing, we employed it in wielding the holystone. "D—n it," some might have said, but "scrape and scrub" was the order, and besides learning some philosophy we had a clean deck again. We note the circumstances, in order that it may be more strongly impressed upon our memory and make us more careful in future when handling indelible fluids. But the music: and what of it?

FIGURE 99. "Six Bells in the Dog Watch." Drawing by Charles Ellery Stedman, Surgeon, U.S. Navy. "Doctor Sawbones' Four Years in the Navy" Sketchbook. Courtesy of the Boston Athenaeum.

We can only say that the crew some few days ago organized a band of Minstrels, and that we have nightly serenades and impromptu dances (Figure 99).[8] Such things serve to make things more pleasant aboard ship, and are worth making a note of. We love music, however rude, and although not much of a dancer we do sometimes "shake a leg," and here we can do so without tearing the dresses or undergoing the scrutiny of the eyes of fair connoisseurs in the art. "Vive le danse!"

Ship Island appears to be a locality in which the scribbler is destined to enjoy himself. While here on a former occasion we spoke of fine weather, fishing, and swimming, as blessings we were enjoying, and now we are adding more amusements, thus making a grateful variety. Of course it is unseasonable to bathe now, but fishing is not only seasonable but highly profitable. Every day brings on board some finny monster—(not specimen). The average weight of the ones now caught is 100 pounds. These are whappers, but with a strong line there is some excitement in hauling them aboard. Besides this, we can now, as then, say we are enjoying delightful weather, and we also have a run on the island merely for the asking. Spring is far advanced here—so far, in fact, that those pests of warm climates we have so often before mentioned, mosquitoes, have already made their appearance. We arrived from Mobile Bay the evening of our last writing, having left our sailor deserters with the Commodore. During our absence the man-of-war yacht *Corpus Christi* arrived from New Orleans. She left again yesterday. No news of importance. They had a funeral on the island yesterday. Two of the negro soldiers were sky-larking[9] with muskets, when one accidentally shot the other. Consequently the black-berrying [burying] party.

---

**FEBRUARY 27, 1863**    Dark, damp and gloomy today. A heavy rain set in about midnight and has been falling all day. A mail steamer heaving in sight early this morning served somewhat to cheer all hands, but only plunged us personally into more gloom, bearing nothing whatever among its mails for us. The steamer was the *Tennessee* from New Orleans. She brought an order from the Admiral recalling Captain Law (Figures 100 and 101) and brought also his successor [Frederick Crocker].[10]

FIGURE 100. Lieutenant Richard L. Law. From the Massachusetts Commandery, Military Order of the Loyal Legion Collection. U.S. Army Military History Institute, Carlisle, Pennsylvania.

FIGURE 101. "The Hero of Galveston [Captain Law] in a Quandery!" Cartoon by Dr. Daniel D. T. Nestell. Handwritten Text Above Figure Reads "Easy, will you. Never be in a hurry! The d____d thing might burst, don't you see! The whole thing should be managed by Law!" Sketch No. 47 by Dr. Daniel D. T. Nestell. Courtesy of the Nestell Collection, Nimitz Library, U.S. Naval Academy, Annapolis, Maryland.

FIGURE 102. Frederick W. Crocker. From Ohio *Military Order of the Loyal Legion of the United States Papers*, vol. 8.

This morning we were under the orders of the one, and, presto, this afternoon we are under the orders of the other. Captain Law mustered all hands at two bells and bade them adieu, at the same time introducing Capt. Crocker (Figure 102) as his successor. The speech was short, but very feeling. We could see that he was loath to leave us, and that he loved us. Perhaps the gloominess of the weather affected his speech, and the dampness of the air dimmed his spectacles; but if his bosom was filled with the same feelings as ours, we cannot think so. We are sorry to lose our gallant captain, and hope his successor may be like him. We saluted him with three rousing cheers as he shoved [off] from the old *Clifton*.

MARCH 4, 1863    "The stormy March has come at last,"[11] and has brought somewhat colder weather than we have been noticing in our last few writings. Still the weather is comfortable enough and duty easy. Boat races in the fleet have become quite the rage, and where we have these, of course there is no lack of excitement. On the 28th ult. a grand affair was to have come off between the winning boat of the *Jackson* and our cutter (Figure 103). It was the main topic of conversation for a week before, and the day was looked anxiously for. It came at last, but the heavy rain that was falling threatened to put a stop to the sport. The *Jackson* also got under way in the morning and did not return until towards evening. While she was yet away the *Vincennes* boats got up a race among themselves, in spite of the rain, and the affair came off with great éclat.[12] When the *Jackson* returned it had cleared up somewhat, and her boat came alongside to fulfill the challenge from us. But after some parleying among the officers, they returned without getting a race. Somebody wasn't satisfied with something—or something else; at least we heard something very much like a groan from the *Jackson*'s boat as she started back again. Perhaps our officers backed down, or perhaps the race was deferred. We cannot tell. Late the same night we were roused from our hammocks and called to quarters, on account of a steamer from New Orleans coming in without showing any signals. Nobody hurt, and everybody ready to receive them in three minutes. The night before we were surprised and disappointed in the same way. Sunday, the 1st passed quietly by as usual, with general muster and fine weather. On Monday we went up the Sound (Figure 104) to take a look around and procure some fresh meat for the fleet. A few poor oxen were purchased at a very

FIGURE 103. Union Sailors in a Ship's Boat. Courtesy of Andrew D. Lytle Collection, Mss. 893, 1254, Louisiana and Lower Mississippi Valley Collections, LSU Libraries, Louisiana State University, Baton Rouge, Louisiana.

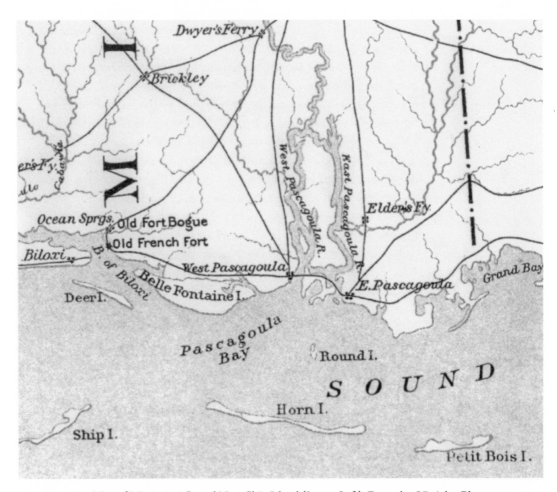

FIGURE 104. Map of Mississippi Sound Near Ship Island (Lower Left). From the OR Atlas, Plate 147.

high rate. Of course the people were Unionists, else we had confiscated them, of course! We returned the same evening. After dark some of the men asked permission to serenade Captain Law, who is yet in the harbor awaiting a steamer North. Permission and a boat was granted, and our Minstrels and some twenty more were soon under the stern of the *Vincennes* "making music like forty." When they had finished, they were informed that Capt. Law was not on board, having gone early in the evening to the *New England*. Quite a sell! Nothing daunted, however, they repeated the concert under the stern of the latter vessel, and were invited on board, thanked, treated, &c., to their hearts' content. The *Union* came in yesterday, but left last evening.

---

MARCH 8, 1863    Dancing, singing and comic performances are still the go, and are the main thing we have to note since our last writing. Strange doings for war times, and yet, as long as they do not interfere with our legitimate business, what harm can come from them, and why should we not indulge in them? "A little foolishness now and then is relished by the best of men," and why should not seamen as well as "the best of men" enjoy themselves? Or as Muggins says,[13] "any other man!" On Thursday evening we had our first performance under canvas, and last night (Saturday) our second. Both were decidedly good and highly gratifying to the audiences. We shall long remember these occasions. On Friday the 6th, we again went up the Sound. When almost within sight of Fort Gaines we discovered a large vessel ashore and on making for her she proved to be the ship *Caroline Nesmith* with part of the 2d Rhode Island cavalry aboard, bound for Ship Island. We succeeded in getting her off, and towed her here. She had been aground two days. The *Tennessee* also arrived, and left same night. Yesterday the bark *Houghton* arrived from Pensacola, with stores for the squadron here.

# 13 *Mississippi Sound*

**MARCH 13, 1863**     We have been as restless as the noted Sala-thiel[1] since our last date, and yet nothing wonderful or surprising has been performed by us. On the 9th we took in a supply of coal at Ship Island, and in the evening, in company with the *Jackson*, proceeded up the Sound as far as Round Island[2] (Figure 105) where we anchored about midnight. In the morning two contrabands came off to us, having run away from their master at Pascagoula, a small town behind the island. They were provided for in accordance with the Emancipation Proclamation,[3] and we

FIGURE 105. Round Island, Mississippi Sound. Sketch No. 31 by Dr. Daniel D. T. Nestell. Courtesy of the Nestell Collection, Nimitz Library, U.S. Naval Academy, Annapolis, Maryland.

proceeded up the Sound as far as Grant's Pass[4] (Figure 106) to reconnoiter. We found the Pass blocked up with sunken vessels and piles, and guarded by an iron battery and three rebel steamers. We lay within gunshot of them for about an hour, but as they did not fire at us we satisfied ourselves with merely a good look.

The next day, the 11th, we paid the steamers another visit, leaving the *Jackson* below, and returned in the afternoon. Having seen a schooner lying near the Pass, and thinking there might be some back-door for her to slip out in the dark, we went up again in the evening to watch her. We had not gone more than half-way when we ran hard aground, in which predicament we remained until morning. As soon as we were afloat again we returned to our rendezvous. The *Jackson* took her turn up there yesterday, and was lucky enough to take a prize. Today we were up again taking a look round, and are now returning. Before we started this morning, two more "cullered individuals" came off from Pascagoula under Uncle Abe's manifesto. Well, let them come! We at first thought ill of the emancipation business, deeming it an abolition scheme, but on calm consideration, the n[egro] appears to us in a new light, viz: As the said individual must, under existing circumstances, be of some benefit to one side or the other, why may we not have them as well as the rebels? If the rebels have them to do their work at home, all the men can be spared for the army. If we free them and garrison our conquered forts with them, we at once add to our force in the field and take away from theirs. This sounds like abolitionism, but it is not—we call it logic.[5]

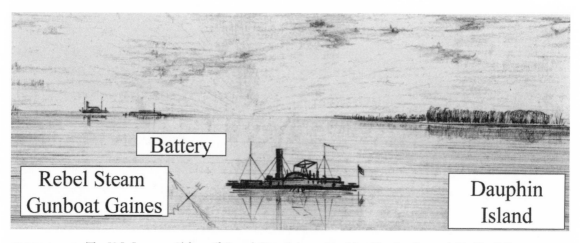

FIGURE 106. The U.S. Steamer *Clifton* off Grant's Pass, July 9, 1863. Identification Boxes Added by Editor Replace Same Text Handwritten by Nestell. Sketch No. 53 by Dr. Daniel D. T. Nestell. Courtesy of the Nestell Collection, Nimitz Library, U.S. Naval Academy, Annapolis, Maryland.

FIGURE 107. "Off Mobile—Shelling a Blockade Runner." From *Harper's Weekly.*

MARCH 16, 1863    We ended up the 13th with quite an exciting circumstance. When about half way back to Round Island, we espied a small sail, which put about as soon as they saw us, whereupon we put on all steam and endeavored to overhaul her. An hour's chase brought us nearly within range, and also very near the shore. We fired six or seven shots from our rifle to bring the vessel to (Figure 107), but as they fell short and she knew the water was too shallow for us to chase her any farther, she kept on. A small bayou soon hid her from our sight and we continued on our course, arriving at Round Island in the evening. The 14th passed off without anything of note transpiring, except that a deserter from Mobile came in. Yesterday we again went up to Grant's Pass and had a look round. The scow-built gunboats we saw there on former visits were not in sight, but their place was supplied by quite a rakish-looking craft of a much larger size. We returned the same evening, and are lying at our old anchorage. The weather is mild and pleasant, and has been so for a week past.

MARCH 22, 1863    St. Patrick's day, the 17th, passed by with its usual storm and sunshine here in Mississippi Sound. In the afternoon a boat hove in sight from Mobile, containing four deserters. We plied for the next two or three days between Round Island and Grant's Pass without anything of note

transpiring. On the 20th we took another prize in the shape of a small schooner, loaded with beans, corn, tobacco, &c., and made prisoners of two men and a bright lad on board her.[6] The same evening we came to Ship Island with our prize, in company with the *Jackson*, where we lay until this morning, when we returned to our old cruising ground. The gunboat *Pinola* was at Ship Island when we left, having come there for repairs. She had brought a small mail, but we must again record the fact that there was nothing for us. As a sort of balance to this sore disappointment, we had a half-day's liberty on the Island. Mem[o]: We have bad news from the Mississippi. Banks has been repulsed at Port Hudson and the frigate *Mississippi* destroyed.[7]

———◦∞◦———

MARCH 26, 1863    Presto! Another change! Our fate is as fickle as the weather we are enjoying, or as a woman's favors. Suddenly, and without notice for preparation, we are shifted from one post to another. We cruised around the Sound waiting the abatement of the equinoxial storm, in order to go outside to the fleet off Mobile Bay until the 24th, on which day we attempted it. We had not proceeded far, however, when a sudden change in the weather caused us to put back again. We put into Pascagoula on our way down, and allowed our prisoners from the prize to communicate with their families in the town, under a flag of truce. After we had come to anchor at Round Island, a sailboat from Ship Island hove in sight, in which was an officer with dispatches for us to proceed immediately to Lake Pontchartrain. We sent our prisoners aboard the *Jackson* and started the same night, arriving at Ship Island at sunrise yesterday morning, and at Fort Pike (Figure 108), on the Rigolettes, in the afternoon, where we are now lying. The scenery around the fort is beautiful, and the fine Spring weather adds much to our enjoyment of it.

# 14 *The Swamps of Louisiana*

MARCH 29, 1863 Unlike Sterne's (we think it was Sterne's) starling, "we can't get in."[1] In his story, he alludes to a bird-cage; in ours, we allude to Berwick Bay. We have been "backing and filling,"[2] and getting aground, and getting off again, since daylight this morning, and now (noon) we are just about as near in as we were then. If we don't run out of fuel, we hope in a few days to record when and how we got in. On the evening of our last writing we received dispatches from New Orleans to proceed here, and started instanter.[3] Although we had a pilot on board, we did not venture out of the Lake that night, but anchored near the outlet. In the morning, soon after we got under way, we picked up a sailboat containing five [Italians], who were fleeing from the draft ordered by Jeff. Davis.[4] We left them at Ship Island, and proceeded on our way here. We had quite a rough passage, but arrived safely. The old *Clifton* is not the sort of boat to be cruising in the Gulf in this weather. Guess our Admiral would think so too, if [he] was in her.

APRIL 1, 1863 In at last, but where we cannot say. Such is the wisdom, or sociability, or something else, among those who ought to know the names of places, that unless school maps are explicit enough to mention the names of all streams and towns in this vast country, one might travel over half of it without knowing even what State he was in.[5] We understood we were to go to Berwick Bay, but it appears from our map that it was Atchafalaya Bay we were lost in. What's in a name, though? The place is beautiful enough with any name, or with no name at all, and we are satisfied that we are inside. Having exhausted all our coal in vain endeavors to find the way into a certain bayou, where we were to cooperate with Gen. [Godfrey] Weitzel from New Orleans, we dropped our anchor, and fitted out a boat expedition on the morning of the 30th, to proceed inside and send one of our steamers to our aid. The same evening a strange steamer hove in sight, and the locality being a suspicious one, of course, it created some excitement. We raked up wood enough to run down to her, with all hands to quarters ready for a fight. She proved to be the *Estrella*,[6] one of our own gunboats, in search of us. We lay alongside of her and took in as much coal as she could spare us, and in the morning followed her in. We met the *Calhoun* inside, also coming out, she having picked up our boat, and thus, with a grand escort, we proceeded up the bayou to Brashear City (Figure 109) arriving at 3 o'clock. Bad news was the first thing that greeted us. One of our steamers, the *Diana* (Figure 110), had been captured by the rebels,[7] some distance further up the bayou, and the greater part of her crew killed, among them some of our *Westfield* shipmates. The bodies of her captain and executive officer had been recovered, and were to be buried that afternoon.[8] It being a military funeral, the marines and sailors of the *Clifton* were invited,

FIGURE 109. The Docks of Brashear City, Louisiana. From *Harper's Weekly*.

and for the first time in our life we took part in a soldier's burial. The marines acted as guard of honor. We buried them in a beautiful orange grove, close by the town. "May they rest in peace."

In the evening we proceeded with the rest of the boats, up the bayou, where the railroad from New Orleans crosses, in order to protect our pickets there, and this morning we returned to Brashear.[9] To say the least of this town, it is a small, neat place, situated at the conjunction of three of the numerous bayous with which this part of the country is intersected, and is connected with New Orleans by a railroad. Opposite to it is another town, called Berwick, in which the rebels often show themselves, notwithstanding the presence of the Union troops and steamers there. The country around is exceedingly rich, and the broad acres and neat and numerous negro quarters bespeak the wealthy planter (Figure 111). The scenery, too, is beautiful, and our trip through the bayous, notwithstanding the danger from the rebels, was truly delightful. Beautiful meadows and lawns, rich fields and shady woods are to be seen on all sides. The lover of picturesque and romantic scenery (Figure 112) would find a paradise here, and if the climate is what it seems to be at present, it is a fine place to spend a life in.[10] But war casts a gloom over all, and it looks as if it will leave its imprint pretty heavily here. There are many troops encamped in and about the town and more arriving daily, and a demonstration will soon be made somewhere.

FIGURE 110. The U.S. Steamer *Diana*. Sketch No. 81 by Dr. Daniel D. T. Nestell. Courtesy of the Nestell Collection, Nimitz Library, U.S. Naval Academy, Annapolis, Maryland.

FIGURE 111. *Clifton* off a Plantation, Bayou Teche. Sketch No. 60 by Dr. Daniel D. T. Nestell. Courtesy of the Nestell Collection, Nimitz Library, U.S. Naval Academy, Annapolis, Maryland.

FIGURE 112. Moss Covered Oak on the Atchafalaya. Sketch No. 54 by Dr. Daniel D. T. Nestell. Courtesy of the Nestell Collection, Nimitz Library, U.S. Naval Academy, Annapolis, Maryland.

FIGURE 113. The Grand Army on the March up the Teche. Sketch No. 56 by Dr. Daniel D. T. Nestell. Courtesy of the Nestell Collection, Nimitz Library, U.S. Naval Academy, Annapolis, Maryland.

APRIL 9, 1863 We have just closed a busy day, and with tired hands and very dirty decks are preparing to coal ship tonight. The grand army of the Southwest crossed the Atchafalaya river [from Brashear to Berwick] today, and the *Clifton* was for the nonce used as a ferryboat. Everything was got over in safety. Some ten thousand troops, including artillery, cavalry and infantry, were transported over. Two war steamers and four transports besides the *Clifton* were engaged in the transportation. The balance of the army, perhaps ten thousand more, will cross tomorrow or next day. Things look as if something desperate is about to take place (Figure 113). The vessels have all been made safe from sharpshooters and otherwise cleared for action. On board of us everything has been bustle and preparation since our arrival here. Iron and cypress logs have added much to the protection of our gunners (Figure 114), and the mounting of an additional rifle has made us still more formidable to the enemy. Several more gunboats are said to be below to aid us. On Saturday evening, the 4th, a false alarm roused all hands from their slumbers, and kept us on the lookout all night. The weather is exceedingly warm, and all hands remarkably healthy.

FIGURE 114. "Old Leach, Gunner's Mate."
Detail from Sketch No. 82 by Dr. Daniel D. T.
Nestell. Courtesy of the Nestell Collection,
Nimitz Library, U.S. Naval Academy,
Annapolis, Maryland.

FIGURE 115. Landing of Federal Forces at Indian Bend, Louisiana, April, 1863.
From *Campfire and Battlefield*.

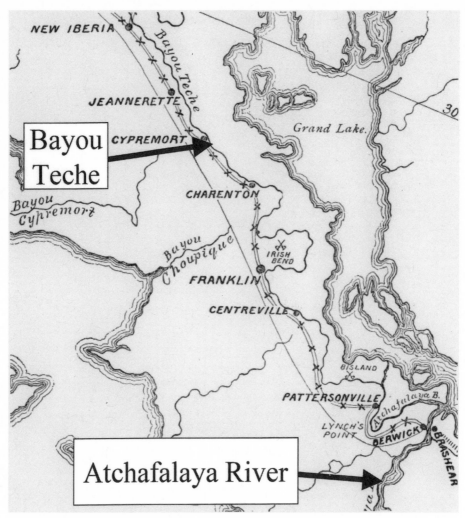

FIGURE 116. Map of Bayou Teche Showing Sites of Irish Bend and Bisland Battles.
From Richard B. Irwin's *History of the Nineteenth Army Corps*.

APRIL 19, 1863   Amid the swamps of Louisiana, we are spending a wet and disagreeable Sunday. Since our last, much of importance has transpired, but we could find no time to scratch a line. On the night of the 11th we took a load of soldiers on board,[11] and with the rest of the fleet and transports proceeded up Chestimacha Lake.[12] Early on Monday morning we landed them, and hardly were they ashore when the rebels attacked them (Figure 115).[13] Our troops soon cleared the place, with but a small loss, and the *Clifton* was dispatched back [down Grand Lake] to proceed up Bayou Teche (Figure 116) to operate with the main body of the army then advancing.[14]

FIGURE 117. U.S.S. *Clifton* on the Teche Removing a Pontoon Bridge at Night. Sketch No. 58 by Dr. Daniel D. T. Nestell. Courtesy of the Nestell Collection, Nimitz Library, U.S. Naval Academy, Annapolis, Maryland.

FIGURE 118. Destruction of the *Queen of the West* on the Atchafalaya River by Union Gunboats (Left to Right, *Estrella*, *Arizona*, and *Calhoun*) on April 14, 1863. From *Harper's Weekly*.

For the next two days our guns were kept talking pretty briskly to the retreating rebel army, whom Gen. [Nathaniel] Banks had started on the run. They made quite a stand near Pattersonville with some of their gunboats and heavy artillery, having the bayou below filled with obstructions and infernal machines. We removed the obstructions (Figure 117) and Banks removed their artillery.[15] We chased them to Newtown, where they destroyed their gunboats [at which point] we returned to Brashear City, arriving on the evening of the 17th. Yesterday we proceeded up here—Atchafalaya river. During our stay up the Teche, the gunboats we left here engaged and destroyed the ram *Queen of the West* (Figure 118).[16]

# 15 *Butte a la Rose*

APRIL 23, 1863     Since our last it has been our lot to go safely through another battle, and today we are lying off the rebel stronghold we have captured. The name of the place we are at is Butte a la Rose and was a place of vast importance to the rebels at Port Hudson and Vicksburg. The fort here (Figure 119)

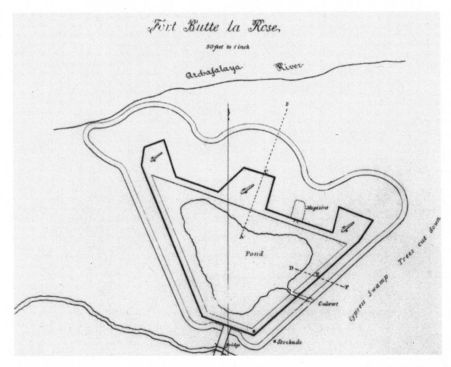

FIGURE 119. Approaches to Fort Butte a la Rose, Louisiana, as surveyed by the U.S. Coast Survey. Library of Congress.

FIGURE 120. Engagement at Butte a la Rose. From *Harper's Weekly*.

is called Fort Burton,[1] and mounted two guns at the time we captured it. On Monday, the 20th, we made the attack (Figure 120), the *Clifton* in the lead, and after a short but decidedly hot contest we drove the gunners from the fort and their gunboats up the bayou.[2] The narrowness of the bayou prevented our capturing their boats although we chased them as far as possible.[3] We took about two hundred prisoners. The *Clifton* was struck several times during the fight and is somewhat disabled. We had one man killed and one wounded. Some cotton, sugar and molasses has fallen into our hands, and undoubtedly some prize money will be due us from this affair. The news from the army acting with us is cheering, their march towards Red River being a succession of victories.

———◦●◦———

APRIL 29, 1863    Still at Brashear. The late fight at Butte a la Rose has damaged us more than we at first thought, and it will yet take several days before we will be fully repaired. In the meantime the crew are having the advantage of our laying up, by having liberty through the town daily. The weather is fine for such pastime and there is much ashore to enjoy and take away one's money. News from our part of the army is still cheering. Success follows success, and every one is in high spirits. Each day, too, brings us more evidence of the magnitude and completeness of our victories up the Teche. Horses and cattle by hundreds, and sugar, molasses and cotton by boatloads, are continually coming in from the captured districts.[4] Contrabands are also becoming plentiful around here.[5] Gen. Banks and staff came down yesterday, and proceeded to New Orleans. We have had news from Charleston, but it is none too cheering. The ironclads, we understand, had to withdraw.[6]

———◦◦◦———

MAY 17, 1863    Sunday, and our day of leisure brings us to our Note-Book, as it was not until the 6th inst. that the repairs to our machinery were finished, and at that time we were under orders to proceed up to Red River and report to Admiral Farragut. We started on the 7th, and after much difficulty arrived within sixty miles of our destination on the next afternoon—the narrowness and tortuous windings of the Atchafalaya preventing our making much headway and damaging our wood-work materially. While lying-to for a few minutes, to make some temporary repairs, the *Sachem* met us from above, with the Admiral on board, proceeding to Brashear. We were informed that our services were not needed up there, as Alexandria had already fallen into our hands without our aid,[7] and we were ordered to return immediately. We arrived at Brashear the next evening, and again set the mechanics to work repairing the old ship, and we are happy to say we are nearly ready for another adventure, fight or anything else that may fall in our way. We have had several mails, but none personally, and news is plent[iful] and contradictory. This place [Brashear] still presents a very business-like aspect, and cotton, sugar and livestock are still daily coming down the river.

———◦◦◦———

MAY 23, 1863    New Orleans once more. Our stay at Brashear was cut short by a peremptory order from headquarters to proceed to Ship Island. This was on the 21st, and accordingly without much regret we weighed anchor and proceeded down the Atchafalaya. We found the weather rather rough when we got outside and the old *Clifton* was tossed about like a washtub in a whirlpool, making some sea-sickness and shaking things up generally. Throughout the night the wind freshened some and for a time things looked as if we were going to have a rough time of it, but a heavy rain coming on somewhat settled the waves and allayed our fears. As it was, however, our rudder was carried away, and we were otherwise slightly damaged; enough so to make us put into the Southwest Pass and telegraph the state of affairs to the Admiral.

We there received orders to come up to the city and repair, which we did—arriving here early this morning. We find things much the same as when last here. There are plenty of merchantmen here, but the war vessels have all gone up to Port Hudson. We anticipate quite a stay here, and expect to have a run through the city.

————◦∞◦————

**MAY 31, 1863** Our anticipation of a stay here at New Orleans seems to have been well founded, and our expectations in regard to a run through the city have been already fulfilled. This much, in regard to the latter at least, we do say, and nothing more. What we *might* say is another thing and belongeth not to diary writing. "Doesticks"[8] wrote his "Trip to Nicaragua," and published it too, but "A Liberty Day in New Orleans," by a U.S. Marine (unless Doesticks joins the corps) has nothing either amusing or instructive in it. Therefore we desist. We can easily remember the various scenes we passed through on that memorable day without recourse to a Note-Book. The repairs to the old *Clifton* are going on rapidly, and we hope in less than a week to be away from the Crescent City. Since our stay here we have been in receipt of a letter from home—the first for five months. "The Era" here speaks of the irregularity of the mails as a great nuisance. We coincide with them. Good news from Port Hudson and Vicksburg is the order of the day, and keeps the city and the military in a constant state of excitement. "Bully for Banks" is the newest and most popular slang in the city and on the shipping.

————◦∞◦————

**JUNE 8, 1863** We are still in New Orleans, although the daily expectation we are in of being ordered away, keeps us from being allowed ashore. Still, to tell the truth, we are not anxious to go. In the warm (or rather hot) weather we deem it much pleasanter to loll about the decks or the cool water, than to run around the streets of a close city—it is a much more economical pastime, at any rate. This afternoon all hands were called to "cheer ship,"[9] in honor of our late Purser, Mr. [J. H.] Carels, who leaves us on account of ill health. It was a hearty cheer, for every man loved him. He was a perfect gentleman, and we couldn't do otherwise. Wish it was somebody else had left instead of him. During the last month or two desertions have been quite numerous from our vessel, and this, with some sickness, leaves us short-handed. When we have filled up once more, with officers and men, we opine it will seem to us like going aboard a new ship. The "somebody else" we have alluded to above is the cause of this. Last Friday we buried one of our shipmates, George Crozier, who died from fever. "Peace to his ashes!" There is no news from up the river and everybody is getting anxious.

# 16 Mobile Bay

JUNE 11, 1863 Today we write in a new latitude, although the place we are at is not altogether unfamiliar. We are in Mississippi Sound again, blockading one of the entrances to Mobile Bay. The evening of our last writing we left New Orleans and the next morning we found ourselves in blue water. We arrived at Ship Island the next afternoon, having an exceedingly smooth run there. The *Pinola*, *Vincennes*, and *Relief* were still lying here, and things were not much changed since our last visit. Having some stores to discharge for the fleet, we laid there until yesterday morning, when we came up to our present position, arriving last evening. The *Jackson* was lying here, and her crew were glad to see us again. This morning we proceeded up as far as advisable on a reconnaissance, returning in the afternoon. The rebels appear to be still further strengthening the batteries at Grant's Pass, and their steamers are still lying inside watching us. We find the weather very pleasant here in comparison to the Mississippi river, and we already realize that our last change is for the better. Fish are also abundant, and the means of catching them are at hand. We had a specimen of them for dinner today.

JUNE 20, 1863 The blockade of Mobile, however rigorously kept up by the fleets outside and in the Sound, seems to be less than a match for the wariness of the rebels, who appear to get in and out of that beleaguered harbor whenever they desire to do so.[1] A few days ago we received information that a steamer had been stolen from New Orleans and run into Mobile, which piece of information was proven correct by a view we had from our end of the blockade of the steamer *Fox*[2] lying snugly inside of Grant's Pass. We yesterday, in company with the *Jackson*, fired a number of rifle shot at her and the battery near which she was lying, causing her to shift position, but eliciting no reply from the fort. This firing appeared to ease our minds somewhat, and we came down the Sound as far as Round Island, stopping at Pascagoula and communicating with that town by a flag of truce. This morning two deserters from the rebel gunboat *Gaines* came in, who stated that the *Fox* ran out again last night, at one of the upper passes leading into the Gulf. On reconnoitering we could see nothing of her, and we have reason to believe the report is true. The weather continues pleasant—bright suns in daytime and thunder showers at night; and the fishing and swimming we enjoy, makes this place truly delightful.

———◦———

**JUNE 27, 1863**    We have just anchored once more outside the range of the battery at Grant's Pass, having arrived from Ship Island. On the evening of the 23rd we left here for the latter place to refill with coal and make some repairs. We experienced quite a heavy rain-squall on the way down, but it did us more good than harm from the fact of the water which fell so copiously being

FIGURE 121. Guard Boat on Picket Duty off Mobile. From *Harper's Weekly*.

fresh and that furnished us by our condenser being very brackish. A mail, fresh beef, potatoes, &c., from the States, and plenty of fishing, made our short stay below quite pleasant. While there, also, the appearance of a small but troublesome rebel craft induced the flag-officer to send a boat expedition in chase of her (Figure 121). Our first and second cutters formed part of the expedition. A chase of twenty-four hours failed to capture her, and our blue-jackets returned much fatigued and very much sun-burned. News from the Mississippi is scarce and not always cheering. On referring back we find that a year ago today we were investing Vicksburg, then the *only* rebel strong-hold on that river. Today it is more formidable than ever,[3] and is not the *only* place not captured. Truly, the rebellion is not yet crushed out. Still, we will here note, that we feel confident it will be.

---

**JULY 5, 1863**   The "Glorious Fourth" passed off without much éclat here in Mississippi Sound. We flew four flags instead of one in honor of the day: we fired a salute of twenty-one guns at noon, and all hands were dressed in white. The blockading fleet outside also fired a salute, the smoke and sound of their guns being very perceptible to us. The rebels, nearly in range of us, did not, of course. In the evening we moved further down, as usual, for the purpose of anchoring for the night, and had the misfortune to get aground. We were soon afloat again, however, and sustained no damage from the mishap. Today we are cruising around, and have just picked up a boat containing two contrabands, who give us the latest rebel news that "General Lee has taken Pennsylvania!"[4] Wonder where he has gone with it—hope not to South Carolina, for, if he has, I'll never go home again. Since our last we have been on a trip to Ship Island, and have had news from the fleet outside that Vicksburg is ours. This is quite cheering, and the spirits of the men have risen several degrees. The weather is very warm, and mosquitoes very plenty. The health of the crew is good, but the tempers of all, owing to the latter, very high.

---

**JULY 12, 1863**   This has been quite a cheerful day, not only to us alone but to all hands. The news of the taking of Vicksburg has been confirmed, and more good news has come, telling us of the fall of Port Hudson.[5] Besides this we are in receipt

FIGURE 122. General Aspect of Horn Island—Mississippi Sound. Sketch No. 70 by Dr. Daniel D. T. Nestell. Courtesy of the Nestell Collection, Nimitz Library, U.S. Naval Academy, Annapolis, Maryland.

of a mail from the North. Several letters for us, one of which states that Lee is actually in Pennsylvania. The contrabands were right; still we do not feel any ways alarmed. We have been busy all day writing home to that effect, and now we finish up by making a note of it here. This morning we made a trip down to Ship Island to take in coal, but were ordered back to our station, the *Jackson* not being ready to relieve us. On our way up we chased a small craft, firing three rifle shots after her, but she eluded us owing to the shallowness of the water. Since our last we have been cruising between Horn Island[6] (Figure 122) and Grant's Pass, nothing of any importance transpiring. The weather is warm, very warm, and every little breeze is a blessing. We must be thankful, however, for a great many of the said breezes. "Blow on," &c.[7]

JULY 21, 1863　The glorious news from every section of the success of our arms keeps all hands in a continual excitement. The reverses of the beginning of the year are entirely overshadowed and forgotten in the successes of the last few months. The end of the rebellion seems much nearer now than then, and it is reasonable to suppose that the next six months will entirely close the concern. Mobile still holds out, and we are still upon the blockade there. Things are the same as ever around here—we watching the rebel gunboats at the battery in the Pass and occasionally running down to Ship Island for coal &c., and the rebel gunboats watching us and occasionally relieving each other ostensibly for the same purpose, coaling. On the 15th we went to Ship Island. On the way down we gave chase to a small sail, and hove her to, after firing three nine-inch shell at her. She contained [an Italian] (what boat here does not?) and three passengers—two men and a lady; the latter very much frightened by the explosion of our shell near their vessel. Ladies not being contraband of war, the flag-officer the next day allowed them to proceed on their way. It is so rare a thing to see a lady on board a man-of-war that we cannot help making a full note of this instance. The same evening volunteers were called for to go on a three days' expedition in search of some piratical launches which were making raids upon our commerce in the Gulf. They returned on the 18th, without having seen the pirates, but making two prizes of small craft, loaded with contraband goods, and burning another in St. Louis Bay.[8] During their absence we coaled ship and made some repairs, and on the 19th we proceeded to our station accompanied by the *Jackson*. On the way we paid a visit to Pascagoula and put a few [Italians] ashore, who had been taken prisoner "inconsistent with the rules of war." We also overhauled a schooner, loaded with women and children, and supplied them with water. Yesterday the *Jackson* picked up two deserters from the rebel fleet, and this morning two from the city of Mobile came to us. They told the usual story of high prices and starvation, and unchristian though it seem, it was good news to all hands. The *Jackson* this morning made a reconnaissance of the battery and was fired upon, but she sustained no damage— the rebels' guns not having the range they calculated.

# 17 The Return to the Teche Country

**JULY 26, 1863**     Aground in Atchafalaya Bay today. On the 23d a dispatch brought us hurriedly off Grant's Pass to Ship Island, where we hurriedly coaled until noon of the 24th, when we put to sea, bound for Berwick Bay, one of our former scenes of "glory." We had a tolerably good passage of thirty-one hours, anchoring last evening in the above Bay, in sight of the steamer *Holly-hock*,[1] also ordered to Berwick, she being aground. This morning we started in, first getting her afloat, and before a pilot boat (then in sight) could reach us, we were hard and fast aground, where there is a possibility of lying until the high tide in the morning. When ordered here we had an intimation of some tall fighting to be expected before reaching Brashear; but we heard from the pilot this morning that the rebels had skedaddled from that vicinity and all is clear. The sun has been somewhat hotter today than we have been used to in the Sound; but the day was in no way tedious, owing to the abundance of fish that we catch around us. Admiral Farragut paid Ship Island a visit on the 23d in the steamer *Tennessee*. He left again on the 24th for Mobile.

---

**JULY 30, 1863**     Pleasant weather for midsummer. Occasional showers and cool evenings are making Berwick Bay quite a charming place to us. Fresh beef and an occasional sprinkling of fine catfish also add much to our delights, and perhaps cause us to keep a better lookout upon the rebels, who are still supposed to be lurking in this vicinity. On the morning of the 27th we succeeded in getting the vessel afloat, and in a few hours we were anchored off

FIGURE 123. "Up the Teche—After Them!" Sketch No. 57 by Dr. Daniel D. T. Nestell. Courtesy of the Nestell Collection, Nimitz Library, U.S. Naval Academy, Annapolis, Maryland.

Brashear City. We found the steamers *Estrella*, *Sachem*, and *Hollyhock* lying here. In the afternoon the entire fleet went up the Teche (Figure 123) on a reconnaissance. At Camp Bisland, about eight miles above, we found quite an army of cavalry, whom we put to flight with a few shells.[2] Coming back by way of the Atchafalaya, the *Estrella* got snagged, and remained so until next morning. Yesterday morning the rebels sent down a flag of truce to exchange some prisoners. Contrabands and deserters are coming to us daily, and report that the rebels are retreating towards Texas. The railroad is being fast repaired,[3] and we expect to have the cars running to New Orleans in about a week.

◄►

AUGUST 2, 1863    The damage done to the railroad by the rebels during their recent reoccupation of this part of the country is not yet fully repaired, and this still keeps us scarce of news and mails from New Orleans. The [newspaper] "Era" made its appearance once this week, one day later than dated, and sold like ice-cream in July. The weather continues fine for this season of the year, occasional showers keeping a pleasant degree of temperature. Contrabands continue coming in daily, with the usual exaggerated accounts of the destitution of the rebels. We have said on a former occasion, "Let 'em come"; but we would much rather pass them along when they do come, than adopt the policy now in vogue here of "shipping" them as fast as they arrive.[4] On the 31st ult. we steered up the river to see how the rebels were getting on, or whether they were erecting any batteries on the Teche. We found nothing but a few cavalry pickets, whom we shelled and caused to scamper. Last evening the transport *Exact* arrived from New Orleans, with stores for the army and some soldiers. The *Hollyhock* left today for New Orleans.

————— ◦∞◦ —————

**AUGUST 10, 1863**    Everything goes on "smoothly as a marriage bell."[5] Nothing new has transpired since our last writing. We were laid up for a few days on the sick list and kept to our hammock, which was a new thing for us; but of course we do not intend to make items of such matters. The weather continues the same—hot with occasional showers. Contrabands are still arriving daily, and we are still enlisting the likely ones among them to fill up our crew. The "Era" comes semi-occasionally and the railroad being now wholly repaired we henceforth expect it regularly and at its

FIGURE 124. Rebel Deserters Coming Into Camp. From *Harper's Weekly*.

published rates. The news from all parts of the country is exceedingly cheering, and the health of our ship very good. This is Brashear news for the last eight days, and although not remarkable items, we are glad we have no worse ones to chronicle. Yesterday morning five rebel cavalry pickets deserted their posts and came into our lines, tying their horses on the opposite side of the river and coming over in a boat (Figure 124). The horses and accoutrements were subsequently sent for. This circumstance, together with the many flags of truce the rebels send, looks as if they were getting uneasy in the Teche country.

---

**AUGUST 16, 1863**    "All quiet along the line."[6] The old *Clifton* has not shifted her anchorage for any hostile purpose since our last date, although we were in to the wharf [at Brashear City] for a day for the purpose of coaling. The transports *Exact* and *Hancox* left for New Orleans a few days ago, thus leaving us and the *Sachem* alone in the waters of Berwick Bay. The railroad to New Orleans is in full operation again, and although there is no great number of troops here, everything looks safe and free from danger. The opening of the railroad brought Gen. Weitzel and staff to Brashear. They arrived on Thursday, the 13th, the *Clifton* firing a salute of fifteen guns in honor to the General, who, in conjunction with his staff, answered us with three very hearty cheers. A most welcome mail has come over the road already, and we hope many more may follow. The weather continues fine, with plentiful showers to keep up a bearable temperature in the daytime, and the evenings are made beautiful by gorgeous sunsets and cool breezes from seaward.

---

**AUGUST 26, 1863**    Flags of truce, daily and semi-daily, are sent by and received from the rebels on the other side of the Atchafalaya. We don't approve of these proceedings— they don't coincide with our ideas of war; but then, our officers think otherwise, and, of course, it is none of our business. *One* flag of truce after each battle is sufficient in our estimation. We didn't like the flags of truce at Galveston, and subsequent events have proved that they were used for no good purpose. Contrabands and deserters from the rebel army are also coming in daily, and from their stories one may well suppose that Jeff's Confederacy is about collapsing. We heartily hope so. On the 21st we had no flag sent us from above, and in the afternoon we went up as far as Pattersonville to rescue the family and effects of a refugee who had come into our lines a few days before. Two companies, from the troops ashore, accompanied us. We were successful, and on the way back we tried our guns against some of the deserted sugar-houses,[7] making the bricks and mortar fly in all directions. The weather is pleasant, but the health of the crew is not so good.

———◇———

SEPTEMBER 1, 1863    Weather clear and bordering a little on the cool. We hope Autumn has commenced at the beginning of the month, instead of waiting for the date usually marked in almanacs. Everything is quiet among the rebels around here, none of them making themselves visible; although last evening a contraband came on board wounded, saying he was shot about half a mile from the opposite shore of the Bay. Still we consider it safe enough to keep the ship encumbered by painting her all over. We take the precaution to "cast loose and provide"[8] at night, however, as usual. On Friday, the 28th, we made a trip up to [Grand] Lake to take a look around, and on our return in the evening we ran on a "sawyer,"[9] which brought us to a stand still quicker than our best bower[10] could have done. The *Sachem* came up to our assistance, and got in the same fix about half a mile from us. After heaving nearly all our coal and water overboard, we got afloat again on Saturday evening, and reached our anchorage, in company with the *Sachem*, without any further damage. Sunday we necessarily occupied in coaling ship, as we expected sailing orders every hour.

———◇———

SEPTEMBER 6, 1863    Our long-expected sailing orders came yesterday morning, and after taking in our stores and ammunition, we weighed our anchor and stood down Berwick Bay for the Gulf. At the time of starting we were under the impression that we were bound for Mobile, the pilot who was sent from New Orleans being known to some of us as a Mobile Bay pilot.[11] But this morning the rumor is prevalent around decks that we are to go to Sabine Pass.[12] Last evening, in crossing the bar, we got aground, and after some six hours hard work we got afloat again without sustaining any damage. We anchored until daylight, when we proceeded outside. We found a gunboat and four transports loaded with troops at anchor waiting for us. After filling up our crew, and taking on board one hundred soldiers of the "glorious 75th New York"[13] to act as sharp-shooters, we took up our course for the Texas coast. Our Mobile pilot has disappeared, and we are all inclined to think that Gen. Banks took quite a Yankee-like way of preventing news of the destination of this expedition from reaching the enemy. If the Texans are not wide awake we, no doubt, will give them a bit of surprise within the next forty-eight hours.

# 18 The Battle of Sabine Pass

SEPTEMBER 9, 1863 We find ourself today in quite a novel position. The few last days have been big with events of interest to us. We have sustained defeat before, and on these occasions we have made short notice of them, but never before now have we been taken prisoner. Were it not that the gallantry of our crew deserves a notice we should say nothing. We will notice this, and then lay aside our Note-Book for awhile. Instead of finding the Texans asleep, as we half suspected we should, we found them ready at their guns to receive us. On the evening of the 7th we anchored off the bar at Sabine [Pass], in conjunction with the rest of the fleet, making twenty-three sail. The troops on the transports were commanded by Generals [William B.] Franklin and [Godfrey] Weitzel, but the number of them we could not ascertain.[1] They were plenty, however, had they been landed, to insure the taking of Sabine Pass. On the morning of the 8th, the *Clifton* crossed the bar and opened fire upon the battery [Fort Griffin] protecting the harbor. After firing some twenty shot we retired over the bar again, the enemy not answering our fire. We ordered the *Sachem* to take the position from which we were firing and anchor until we again came up. In about an hour we again crossed the bar and were soon followed by our steam transports. We understood it was the intention of the commander of the land forces to land his troops under the fire of the gunboats, when, all things being ready, a combined attack would be made. The *Clifton* was to lead the attack, and all hands were glad for an opportunity of showing the troops that sailors could fight as well as soldiers. About half past two a movement was made (Figure 125), and our brave captain gave his final orders for a close engagement. We fired awhile at long range, our shell appearing to burst with great precision over the battery, but no answer was returned. The *Sachem* steamed ahead of us, and on coming in line with a suspicious looking stake on the opposite shore, was opened upon with great fury by the battery. Before she had moved two lengths her boiler was struck, killing and scalding a large number of her crew, and disabling the vessel. Seeing this, we hastened to get between the disabled ship and the battery, and thus draw the fire upon ourselves and fight the battery until she was towed off. But the other vessels (either through timidity or incapacity to steam fast enough) were too slow for Capt. Crocker, and in endeavoring to run the gauntlet we got aground within four hundred yards of the battery.

Before we could extricate ourselves from this difficulty a shot struck our steam-chest, leaving us helpless (Figure 126). But at it we went, "hammer and tongs,"[2] with the battery, although but four of our guns could be brought to bear in the position in which we laid, the fourth one being made of use after tearing away the ship's side and making a new port. We have been in several battles since our enlistment, but never have we been in one where we saw displayed so much coolness and calm courage. From the captain to the powder boys, with but one exception,[3] every one stood by his quarters until

FIGURE 125. The Attack on Sabine Pass, September 8, 1863, Sketched by Eyewitness James A. Ferguson, Co. A, First Indiana Artillery. From *Harper's Weekly*.

FIGURE 126. The Disabling and Capture of the Federal Gunboats *Sachem* (Right) and *Clifton* (Left) in the Attack on Sabine Pass, Texas, September 8, 1863. From *The Soldier in Our Civil War*, vol. 2.

we were compelled to strike our flag. Had this one exception been on board of one of the gunboats which were to have supported us, but did not, he would have been well mated. We will mention no names, but we will make a note of this circumstance. Shortly after the firing ceased we were boarded by the officers from the battery, who ordered us aboard one of their own steamers, first, however, allowing us to take what clothing belonged to us. The *Sachem* also surrendered. The same evening we left Sabine Pass, and today we are in Beaumont, some eighty miles northward. We get a tolerably good ration thus far, and although not so substantial as Uncle Sam's, yet we are thankful we have an appetite for it. May the appetite long continue, as there is no doubt we shall long need it.

# 19 Letters from Prison

## Letter from the Author of the Yankee Note-Book

Camp Groce, October 3, 1863

[To] W[illard] Richardson, Editor—Dear Sir:

I notice that the *Tri-Weekly News* is publishing a series of notes from a "Yankee Note-Book," the two last ones (Sept. 30 and Oct. 2) of which I have purchased. I am unable to procure the first number, and am very anxious to do so, and also to insure the forthcoming ones to the end. If you could oblige me by directing the first number, and the balance after Oct. 2, to me at Camp Groce, I should be very happy to receive them.[1] I enclose five dollars. My name was, I believe, only on the cover of the book, and may have been erased; therefore, I think it may be proper that I should let you know that I am the writer of those notes. I am sorry that they fell into your hands; but as you are making use of them, I shall be much obliged if I get a printed copy in lieu of the original notes.

Respectfully yours,
HENRY O. GUSLEY

[Reply from the Editor]

We shall most cheerfully comply with the above request, returning the five dollars, as we consider the manuscript an ample equivalent for the printed copy of it. We omitted the name thinking its publication might operate prejudicially to the author.

## Letter from the Author of the Yankee Note-Book

Camp Groce, October 13, 1863

[To] W. Richardson, Esq.—Dear Sir:

The numbers of your *News*, for which I asked, came duly to hand.[2] The courteous and gentlemanly manner in which you have treated me in respect to them, demands that I should again thank you. Since my sojourn in this State, I have universally found Texans to be a polite and generous people. My position as a prisoner of war neither demanded nor deserved the display of these virtues, and therefore my admiration of them may be candidly expressed. The last act of yours in complying with my request for a favor from my captors has heightened my respect for your State at least.

The letter accompanying the papers I have read and duly considered. Your request for me to send you the balance of my notes up to the time of our capture I can comply with. Thus far I may prove that I am under obligations to you. But, however much I would like to avail myself of the opportunity to express my views upon the present war and the causes which led to it, my position as a sworn soldier of the Federal Government debars me from doing so. Your supposition that, as a "freeman having still the constitutional right to express my opinions," I can do so, is erroneous. A soldier is not entitled to the free expression of his opinions, nor is he allowed to discuss and comment upon the actions of his government. The late amendments to the "Act for the better government of the navy of the United States" was decisive on this point, and I should make myself amenable to the laws which I have accepted for my government whilst in the U.S. Navy, did I dare utter anything against the present Administration. This franchise belongs only to those in authority, and my duty teaches me to grant it to them without a murmur. What opinions, founded upon experience, I have expressed in my Note-Book, can scarcely be evidence against me, as they were not written for publication, nor do you give them to the world as the opinions of the crew or corps to which I belonged; but it must be obvious to you, that were I to venture any farther I would be treading upon dangerous ground. That I hold the same opinions regarding the right or the wrong of slavery and the doctrine of State Sovereignty as you have seen proper to express privately to me, I may say I do, and in this the National Democratic party and conservatives North and South agree with us. These men did not and would not agitate this question; they endeavored to allay the storm when-

ever it was raised, knowing as they did how fraught with destruction to the Union it was should it be pushed to extremes. But these
patriots were too few for the numerous class of crafty politicians
who saw in its agitation an opportunity for setting the fanatics of
both sections at each other's throats, and by this means advance their
own interests. They attained their object and the South seceded.
The right of secession was not and *is not now* admitted by the North.
Herein, too, the National Democratic party (or a majority of them)
modify the doctrine of State Sovereignty. The Union is paramount
to everything with them, and in this they coincide with the Administration. You of the South continue to think differently, and argument
is useless. We must remain enemies until the Union is restored, and
be it with slavery extended or entirely exterminated, it is a "consum-
mation devoutly to be wished."[3]

Believe me, then, that the great mass of the people of the North
do not uphold the Administration on the principle of abolishing
slavery, but that the restoration of the Union is the grand incen-
tive; and while such is the fact, every nerve and every sinew will be
strained to bring about a victorious end.—Would to Heaven that
the blood already spilled was a sufficient sacrifice for this great result.

Hoping that my reasons for not accepting your kind offer may
prove satisfactory, and that you will excuse any indiscreet remark
I may have made, I remain, your obedient servant.

HENRY O. GUSLEY

# Notes

## Introduction

1. The beginning section of the "Yankee Note-Book" was published in the *Galveston Tri-Weekly News* on September 28, 1863. The remainder of the Note-Book was published in daily installments (frequently repeated the next day) essentially without interruption for the next two months. The concluding section was published in the edition of November 20, 1863.

2. This biographical information is taken from Gusley's Official Service Record in Record Group 127 of the Records of the U.S. Marine Corps and the pension file relating to his widow, Sarah Gusley, in the National Archives. Navy Dependents Certificate No. 3324 (NWC 0002628).

3. *Lancaster Daily Intelligencer*, November 3, 1880.

4. Note-Book entries of October 9 and November 2, 1862, and letter to W. Richardson (Chapter 19 herein) dated October 13, 1863.

5. Note-Book entries of May 4, September 20, and December 2, 1862.

6. *(Rochester) Union and Advertiser*, December 19, 1884.

7. This biographical information on Dr. Nestell is taken from the Dr. Daniel D. T. Nestell papers, manuscript collection no. 310, Nimitz Library, United States Naval Academy, Annapolis, Maryland.

8. The 1878 *Catalogue of the Library of the Boston Athenaeum* includes Nestell's 1856 publication, "A Brief Treatise on the Diseases of the Respiratory Organs."

9. Naval History Division, Navy Department, *Dictionary of American Naval Fighting Ships* (Washington, D.C.: Government Printing Office, 1959; reprinted with corrections, 1970), hereinafter DANFS, 1:18.

10. F. Crocker to G. Welles, Edgarton, Massachusetts, April 21, 1865, *Official Records of the Union and Confederate Navies in the War of the Rebellion* (Washington, D.C.: Government Printing Office, 1905), hereinafter ORN, 20:547.

11. D. D. T. Nestell to G. Welles, Navy Yard, New York, May 5, 1865, 20 ORN 549–551.

12. The information relating to Dr. Nestell's dismissal from the Navy, his postwar career, and his death is taken from Dr. Nestell's pension application (Certificate No. 20479) and that of his widow, Maria (Certificate No. 14438), which fill a lengthy file in the U.S. Navy's pension records at the National Archives and Records Administration in Washington, D.C.

13. David S. Heidler and Jeanne T. Heidler, eds., *Encyclopedia of the American Civil War* (Santa Barbara, California: ABC-CLIO Inc., 2000), 3:1253 (entry on "Marines, U.S.," by Michael S. Davis). The reader wishing to know more about the Marines in the Civil War should read the definitive four-volume work on this subject,

David M. Sullivan, *The United States Marine Corps in the Civil War* (Shippensburg, Pennsylvania: White Mane, 1997–2000).

14. Allan R. Millett, *Semper Fidelis: The History of the United States Marine Corps* (New York: Free Press, 1980), 93.

15. George Riddell to Mother, Fort Jackson, Mississippi River, April 16, 1862, George Riddell Papers, Marine Corps University Research Archives, Gray Research Center, Marine Corps Combat Development Command, Quantico, Virginia; hereinafter Riddell Papers.

16. George Riddell to Mother, off Staten Island, February 19, 1862, Riddell Papers.

17. Note-Book entries for May 6, June 1, and October 21, 1862.

18. Note-Book entry for June 19, 1862.

19. Craig L. Symonds, *The Naval Institute Historical Atlas of the U.S. Navy* (Annapolis, Maryland: Naval Institute Press, 1995), 82–84.

20. Born in Chester, Pennsylvania, David Dixon Porter (1813–1891) was the son of Commodore David Porter, a naval hero in the American Revolution and the War of 1812. After serving on blockade duty in the Gulf of Mexico in 1861, David Dixon Porter proved instrumental in convincing the Navy to consider a plan to capture New Orleans. Then, when his plan was adopted, Porter was placed in command of the Mortar Flotilla that was an integral part of that plan. Kenneth E. Thompson Jr., *Civil War Commodores and Admirals: A Biographical Directory* (Portland, Maine: Thompson Group, 2001), 119–121.

21. G. Welles to D. D. Porter, Navy Dept., February 10, 1862, 18 ORN 25.

22. George W. Brown, "The Mortar Flotilla, and Its Connection with the Bombardment and Capture of Forts Jackson and St. Philip," *Military Order of the Loyal Legion of the United States (New York Commandery)*, vol. 1 (1891; reprinted, Wilmington, North Carolina: Broadfoot Publishing, 1992), 20:173.

23. David D. Porter, "The Opening of the Lower Mississippi," in *Battles and Leaders of the Civil War, Grant-Lee Ed.* (1887; reprinted, Harrisburg, Pennsyl-

vania: Archive Society, 1991), hereinafter *Battles and Leaders*, 2:26.

24. Brown, "Mortar Flotilla," 177.

25. Ibid., 174.

26. "Scenes on the Lower Mississippi," *Harper's Weekly* 6, no. 294 (August 16, 1862): 523.

27. Brown, "Mortar Flotilla," 176.

28. ORN [Series 2], 1:238.

29. Ibid., 59.

30. George Riddell to Brother John, Baltimore, Maryland, March 4, 1862, Riddell Papers.

31. A. A. Hoehling, *Damn the Torpedoes! Naval Incidents of the Civil War* (Winston-Salem, North Carolina: John F. Blair, 1989), 28.

32. Born in Knoxville, Tennessee, David Glasgow Farragut (1801–1870) was the stepbrother of David Dixon Porter. When the Civil War erupted in 1861, Farragut was first assigned to administrative duty. But when the Gulf Blockading Squadron was divided at the beginning of 1862, Farragut was selected to command the western half as Flag Officer of the West Gulf Blockading Squadron. His first assignment in this command was to lead his squadron up the Mississippi River and capture New Orleans. Thompson, *Civil War Commodores and Admirals*, 57–62.

33. Porter, "Opening of the Lower Mississippi," 2:29.

34. William T. Meredith, "Farragut's Capture of New Orleans," in *Battles and Leaders*, 2:70.

35. George Riddell to Mother, Southwest Pass of the Mississippi River, April 1, 1862, Riddell Papers.

36. D. D. Porter to G. Welles, Passe a l'Outre, March 18, 1862, 18 ORN 72.

37. Eugene B. Canfield, "Porter's Mortar Schooners," *Civil War Times Illustrated* 6, no. 6 (October 1967): 30–31.

38. Letter from E. Higgins to D. Porter, April 4, 1872, quoted in Porter, "Opening of the Lower Mississippi," 2:36

39. J. Harris to F. H. Gerdes, South West Pass, Mississippi River, May 4, 1862, 18 ORN 393–394.

40. Meredith, "Farragut's Capture of New Orleans," in *Battles and Leaders*, 2:71–72.

41. Edwin Forbes, *Thirty Years After: An Artist's Memoir of the Civil War* (Baton Rouge: Louisiana State Univer-

sity Press, 1993), xi–xii (introduction by William J. Cooper Jr.).

42. Note-Book entry of June 19, 1862.

43. Michael J. Bennett, *Union Jacks: Yankee Sailors in the Civil War* (Chapel Hill: University of North Carolina Press, 2004), 160.

44. Note-Book entry of September 25, 1862.

45. Note-Book entry of February 17, 1863.

46. Note-Book entry of March 13, 1863.

47. Dennis J. Ringle, *Life in Mr. Lincoln's Navy* (Annapolis, Maryland: Naval Institute Press, 1998), 14.

## Galveston Tri-Weekly News *Introduction to "A Yankee Note-Book"*

1. As described by Gusley in his Note-Book's last entries, the steamer *Clifton* (on which Gusley served as a member of the Marine Guard beginning in January 1863 and on which he was eventually captured) was forced to surrender at the Battle of Sabine Pass on September 8, 1863. At that battle, a force of fewer than fifty Confeder- ates under the command of Lieutenant Richard "Dick" Dowling defeated a Union invasion fleet including four shallow-draft gunboats. *Clifton* was the flagship of this unsuccessful expedition to Texas. *See* Edward T. Cotham, Jr., *Sabine Pass: The Confederacy's Thermopylae* (Austin: University of Texas Press, 2004), 139–142.

## Chapter 1

1. The *Posthumous Papers of the Pickwick Club*, published by Charles Dickens in 1838, states that the origins of the club that is the book's subject are obscure. The book uses the literary device, uncommon in books of the day, of starting in the midst of the action and forcing the reader to gradually decipher what is happening as the plot unfolds. Gusley's diary is similar in that it begins about three months after his departure from Staten Island, New York, on board *Westfield*.

2. These forts, located on the Mississippi River below New Orleans, were passed under fire by a naval force under the command of Commodore David Glasgow Farragut on the night of April 24, 1862. The forts were not formally surrendered by the Confederates until April 28, 1862.

3. On April 13, 1862, the steamers of the Mortar Flotilla were protecting a Coast Survey party that was surveying possible approaches and channels in connection with the naval attack that Farragut was about to launch on the forts below New Orleans. When two Confederate gunboats got too close to the Union survey team, *Westfield* and *Harriet Lane* were ordered forward to see if they could reach the rebel steam- ers with their rifled guns. Commander William B. Renshaw (the captain of *Westfield*) claimed that as a result of the subsequent long-range bombardment, the Confederate gunboat *Defiance* was so crippled that it later was sunk by her crew. W. B. Renshaw to D. D. Porter, Mississippi River, May 5, 1862, 18 ORN 389.

4. Named after the niece of President James Buchanan, the side-wheel steamer *Harriet Lane* had been built in 1857 for the Treasury Department, where it served as a revenue cutter. It served as Commodore Porter's flagship during the operations at New Orleans. DANFS 3:250–251; David P. Marvin, "The Harriet Lane," *Southwestern Historical Quarterly* 39, no. 1 (July 1935): 15–20.

5. The "hurricane deck" was the uppermost deck on a steamship. The word "sentry-go" that Gusley uses was a recognized military term in the nineteenth century for what today we would call sentry "duty." It apparently originated from the actual command given to a new sentry to go and replace the man being relieved. *Compact Edition of the Oxford English Dictionary* (Oxford, England: Oxford University Press, 1971), hereinafter OED, 1351, 2730.

6. Almost as soon as the American colonies were settled, the game of nine-pins became a popular form of recreation. But when it became the object of a great deal of gambling, some colonies chose to outlaw it. The result was that the game of nine-pins was modified by clever proponents to ten-pins (not technically illegal under the literal terms of the statute), and it is from this revised game that modern American bowling developed. To break a tie between competing bowlers there were a variety of possible procedures; the "old and new" method mentioned by Gusley involved going back through the last few frames to determine which player had won those frames, and if no winner was determined based on looking at past performance, then the scoring started again with a new additional frame. What Gusley is suggesting to the reader with his bowling analogy is that he is now going to jump back out of sequence and describe the capture of New Orleans before returning to a description of current events.

7. John A. Gusley, born in 1836, according to census records, was a sergeant in the Fifty-second Indiana Infantry.

8. Fort Heiman (referred to as "Hyman" in Gusley's journal) was an auxiliary fortified position in southwestern Kentucky that was designed to support Fort Henry across the Tennessee River. The fort was still uncompleted when Fort Henry fell to the Union on February 6, 1862. Robert B. Roberts, *Encyclopedia of Historic Forts: The Military, Pioneer, and Trading Posts of the United States* (New York: Macmillan, 1988), 312.

9. The Fifty-second Indiana Infantry was mustered in at the beginning of February 1862. The regiment participated in the Union expedition to capture Fort Donelson during February 13–15, 1863, and fought in the battle on February 15 as part of the Union left wing. *Supplement to the Official Records of the Union and Confederate Armies* (Wilmington, North Carolina: Broadfoot, 1995), vol. 17, serial no. 29: 462–484.

10. Today called Pilottown (one word), this was, as its name suggests, the town from which ships picked up or dropped off river pilots, who were essential to the navigation of the treach-erous waters of the Mississippi River from its mouth to New Orleans. At the place where the Mississippi entered the Gulf of Mexico, the river deposited its sediment in vast sandbars, leaving only a series of fan-shaped passes through which oceangoing ships could navigate. The town Gusley refers to as Pilot Town was just below the point where these passes converged (referred to at the time as the "head of the passes").

11. Gusley was considerably more impressed with Pilot Town than was the artist from *Harper's Weekly* who visited it in late 1861. Claiming that his drawing showed "every miserable building in the place," the artist observed that "Pilot Town is an old and dilapidated place of a few hundred inhabitants, chiefly pilots and their families, fishermen, and oystermen." "The Fight at the Southwest Pass," *Harper's Weekly* 5, no. 258 (December 7, 1861): 779.

12. As Gusley suggests, mosquitoes were more than a simple nuisance. They carried diseases, including yellow fever, which could and did prove fatal. One historian has observed that the "disease-carrying, pesky little mosquito proved to be a greater adversary to the Union sailors than the Confederate navy." Ringle, *Life in Mr. Lincoln's Navy*, 116.

13. *Westfield* left New York on February 22, 1862, accompanied by the steamers *Clifton, R. B. Forbes,* and *John P. Jackson*. Due to a series of storms, the ships later became separated and suffered substantial damage. W. B. Renshaw to D. D. Porter, South West Pass of the Mississippi River, April 1, 1862, 18 ORN 93.

14. "The Narrows" is the strait in southeast New York between Brooklyn and Staten Island that connects Upper and Lower New York Bay. The Narrows is today spanned by the Verrazano-Narrows Bridge, one of the longest suspension bridges in the world.

15. As Gusley's reference to dressing "tidily in clean clothes" reflects, the typical Sunday routine on a Union naval vessel involved personnel inspection by the commanding officer, followed by religious services. This typically involved the captain's reading of the Episcopalian rituals. There was a tremendous shortage of chaplains in the Gulf of Mexico. Indeed, during the spring of 1863, not a single ship in the Gulf reported having

a chaplain on board. Ringle, *Life in Mr. Lincoln's Navy*, 89.

16. In nautical terminology, the act of doubling is accomplished when a cape or point is passed or rounded so that the ship's course is doubled or bent back on itself. OED, 791.

17. Port Royal, South Carolina, which was captured by the Union in November 1861, served as an important base of operations throughout the war for U.S. Navy blockaders and warships. Its location between the two important Confederate ports of Charleston and Savannah made it a very strategic site.

18. When the war broke out, the inhabitants of Key West strongly favored the Confederate cause. But the presence of U.S. forces at the Key West Naval Base and the Key West Barracks enabled the Union to maintain control of the city, which became the center of a strong military presence that kept it in Federal hands throughout the war. Patricia L. Faust, ed., *Historical Times Illustrated Encyclopedia of the Civil War* (New York: Harper & Row, 1986), 416 (entry on "Key West, Florida, Union Department of," by Edward J. Longacre).

19. Named after President Zachary Taylor, Fort Taylor was constructed off Key West beginning in 1845 at the site of a former naval base. Built in the shape of a three-tiered trapezoid, it was situated on a sandy shoal about a quarter-mile from the shore, where it commanded all of the water approaches to Key West. Boasting one of the largest existing inventories of Civil War cannons, today it is a National Historic Landmark. Roberts, *Encyclopedia of Historic Forts*, 209–210.

20. Where the Mississippi River enters the Gulf of Mexico, the river's huge delta is divided by a series of channels or passes. The outer one, extending in a more or less easterly direction, was called the Pass (or "Passe") a l'Outre, meaning "the outer pass."

21. David D. Porter, commanding the Mortar Flotilla, wrote in his official report that too much praise could not possibly be awarded to *Westfield* and the other ships in the steamer division because "in the end the united power of these vessels succeeded in getting over the bar the heaviest vessels that ever entered the Mississippi River." Detailed Report of D. D. Porter, Forts Jackson and St. Philip, April 30, 1862, 18 ORN 362.

22. Captain Robert Bennet Forbes (1804–1889) was part of a network of prominent families who helped shape maritime and trading history during the golden era of sailing ships. Forbes was particularly influential in promoting trade with China. *R. B. Forbes*, the twin-screw steamer named for him, was built in 1845. It was acquired by the U.S. Navy at Boston in August 1861. The steamer was ordered to join the South Atlantic Blockading Squadron in late October. Sailing on October 29, 1861, *Forbes* participated in the capture of Forts Walker and Beauregard at Port Royal. Following damage to its port shaft and propeller, *Forbes* was towed to New York by the steamer *Atlantic*. Decommissioned for repairs, it was recommissioned in February 1862 and ordered to join the Mortar Flotilla below New Orleans. Caught in a gale off Cape Henry, however, *Forbes* was driven ashore and wrecked. The grounded steamer was then burned to prevent capture by Confederate forces. DANFS, 6:9.

23. Built in Brooklyn, New York, in 1860, *John P. Jackson* was a 192-foot-long ferryboat that had been purchased by the U.S. Navy from the Jersey City Ferry Co. in 1861. Ibid., 3:538.

24. A coal whip was a pulley apparatus used to rapidly load coal into a ship's hold, and the men who operated it were sometimes referred to as "coal-whippers." OED, 448–449. "Coal-heavers" were the lowest rating of men in the engineering division on a ship. They were in charge of shoveling coal into the steam boiler's furnace. It was hot, miserable work and was often assigned to black crewmen. When the ship was "coaling," or taking on coal supplies, other members of the ship's crew, including the Marines, were enlisted to assist with the transfer of thousands of bags of coal into the chutes leading to the bunker where the coal was stored. This process spread coal dust throughout the ship, which then had to be cleaned. Ringle, *Life in Mr. Lincoln's Navy*, 47, 52; Bennett, *Union Jacks*, 35.

25. Sailing ships in the U.S. Navy had historically been classified based upon the number and placement of

masts and sails. By the time of the Civil War, when steamers were becoming more common, the term "frigate" referred to a large ship with twenty-eight to forty-four guns, usually mounted on two decks. A "sloop-of-war" was a cruiser that mounted eighteen to thirty-two guns on one deck. A "gunboat" was a smaller or lighter draft vessel carrying one or more guns of heavy caliber. James M. Morris and Patricia M. Kearns, *Historical Dictionary of the United States Navy* (Lanham, Maryland; Scarecrow Press, 1998), 101, 117, 289.

26. In a letter to Navy headquarters in Washington, Commander David Porter wrote, "No one did more execution with their guns than [*Westfield*'s commander] did with his hundred pound rifle which he never missed an opportunity of firing when he had the time to devote to the enemy." Extract of letter to G. Welles, U.S. Steamer *Harriet Lane*, Mississippi River, May 6, 1862, W. B. Renshaw Civil War Letters, Department of Rare Books and Special Collections, Rush Rhees Library, University of Rochester, Rochester, New York.

27. The commander of *Westfield* claimed after this encounter that fire from his guns had broken the shaft of the Confederate gunboat *Defiance*, leading the rebels to sink it. W. B. Renshaw to D. D. Porter, Mississippi River, May 5, 1862, 18 ORN 389. Confederate reports, however, state that there was no damage to that vessel and reflect that *Defiance* was sunk well after the engagement only to prevent it from falling into the hands of the enemy. J. K. Mitchell to S. R. Mallory, Greensboro, North Carolina, August 19, 1862, 18 ORN 297.

28. A Marine on *Clifton* confirmed Gusley's opinion, writing home to his mother that the bombardment was "one of the grandest sites ever witnessed." George Riddell to Mother, New Orleans, May 1, 1862, Riddell Papers.

29. Construction of this fort, named after Andrew Jackson, began in 1822 and was largely completed by 1832. It was built as a star-shaped pentagon, with walls rising twenty-five feet above the waters of a moat that completely encircled it. There were only about sixty-nine guns at the fort at the time of the battle with Farragut's fleet. Roberts, *Encyclopedia of Historic Forts*, 340.

30. The quoted verse is from "The Burial of Sir John Moore after Corunna" by Charles Wolfe (1817). Sir John Moore (1761–1809) was a British general who was in command of the army in Spain during the Peninsular War. When the French captured Madrid, Moore led a desperate winter retreat to the coast at Corunna. Moore was killed during the last stages of this retreat while bravely conducting a rearguard action in order to buy enough time for his men to escape.

31. Located across the river from Fort Jackson, Fort St. Philip was actually the earlier of the two, its construction having begun in 1792. Roberts, *Encyclopedia of Historic Forts*, 352. General Benjamin Butler led his troops to the rear of that fort in order to cut off any potential Confederate retreat from that position. As he later summarized the experience, "To get there I myself waded in water above my hips for nearly two miles—which was not unsafe but unpleasant." Benjamin F. Butler, *Butler's Book* (Boston: A. M. Thayer & Co., 1892), 1:368.

32. Commander Porter was enthusiastic about the part that *Westfield* and its commander, William B. Renshaw, had played in capturing New Orleans. "No one during this rebellion," he wrote to naval authorities in Washington, "has performed better service or done more to advance the cause for whom we have been fighting." Recognizing *Westfield*'s limitations as a fighting ship, Porter noted, "Frail as his vessel is, [Renshaw] has never hesitated to place her under the fire of forts Jackson and St. Philip or anything else when opportunities occurred for doing so." Extract of Letter to Hon. G. Welles, U.S. Steamer *Harriet Lane*, Mississippi River, May 6, 1862, W. B. Renshaw Civil War Letters, Department of Rare Books and Special Collections, Rush Rhees Library, University of Rochester, Rochester, New York.

33. In his account of the battle, Commander Porter made more precise calculations, estimating that the total number of shells fired at the Confederate forts was 16,800, about 2,800 every 24 hours. He estimated that the distance from the leading mortar schooner to Fort Jackson was about 2,850 yards. Porter, "Opening of the Lower Mississippi," 32, 38.

## Chapter 2

1. One of Mississippi's barrier islands, Ship Island was used by the U.S. Navy as the staging area for the attack on New Orleans. Because of its excellent natural harbor, Ship Island served the Union blockading fleet as a supply and repair facility. Strategically, its location a little over ten miles off the Mississippi coast was within easy distance of New Orleans, the entrance to the Mississippi River, Mobile, and Pensacola. As a reporter described it to a Northern newspaper, "Ship Island is somewhat undulating, and extends in a slight curve about seven miles east-northeast and west-southwest. At West Point (the western end) where the fort is located, the island is little more than an eighth of a mile wide, and is a mere sand spit, utterly barren of grass or foliage of any kind. . . . The whole island contains a fraction less than two square miles of territory. . . . The island possesses a very superior harbor, into which [a ship drawing] nineteen feet can be carried at ordinarily low water." "Our War Illustrations," *Harper's Weekly* 6, no. 262 (January 4, 1862): 2.

2. This group of ships together with some other steamers like *Sachem* comprised the "Steamer Division" of the Mortar Flotilla in the spring of 1862. F. H. Gerdes, "Reconnaissance Near Fort Morgan and Expedition in Lake Pontchartrain and Pearl River, By the Mortar Flotilla of Captain David D. Porter, U.S.N.," *Continental Monthly* 4, no. 3 (September 1863): 269.

3. Fort Gaines, named after American General Edmund Pendleton Gaines, was constructed over a long period of time beginning in the 1850s on the site of an earlier fort. A regular pentagonal bastioned work, it was seized by the Confederates in 1861. Roberts, *Encyclopedia of Historic Forts*, 5. Fort Morgan, named for American Revolution General Daniel Morgan, was designed as a five-pointed star fort. Construction on the brick fort began in 1820 and was completed in about 1834. Ibid., 10–11.

4. Historian Arthur W. Bergeron Jr. has correctly observed that "Mobile on the eve of the Civil War was the leading city of Alabama and one of the most important cities in the South." Arthur W. Bergeron Jr., *Confederate Mobile* (Baton Rouge: Louisiana State University Press, 1991), 3.

5. Porter had originally intended to anchor his mortars at specified distances from the Confederate forts at the entrance to Mobile Bay and to carefully chart the most effective positions for firing on those forts. However, a severe northeast storm raged for a day or two, sweeping the sailing vessels in the fleet far out to sea and leading ultimately to the cancellation of the exercise. Gerdes, "Reconnaissance Near Fort Morgan," 269.

6. Although Gusley was unaware of it, the Mortar Flotilla's demonstration at the entrance to Mobile Bay on May 7 had one important result. It was this action that caused the Confederates to evacuate and destroy the Navy Yard at Pensacola in order to concentrate their forces at Mobile. T. M. Jones to J. H. Forney, Mobile, May 14, 1862, *The War of the Rebellion: A Compilation of the Official Records of the Union and Confederate Armies* (Washington, D.C.: Government Printing Office, 1882), hereinafter *OR*, 6:660; Bergeron, *Confederate Mobile*, 55.

7. The blockade runner mentioned by Gusley used stealth and cunning to enter the bay in the midst of the Union blockaders. It came in during the late afternoon and calmly anchored near *Westfield*. The Union sailors believed it was one of the mortar schooners. It even gave signals during the night as if it were part of the Union fleet. But when dawn came, the blockaders were embarrassed to see that the schooner had slipped away from the fleet during the night and had instead anchored safely within range of the guns of the Confederate fort. George Riddell to Brother John, Ship Island, May 19, 1862, Riddell Papers.

8. Located in St. Tammany Parish, Louisiana, Madisonville is on the north shore of Lake Pontchartrain, opposite the city of New Orleans. When the mortar steamers came within view of Madisonville, they noticed a large white flag hoisted above the trees. Puzzled by this strange signal, the naval officers

eventually decided that it did not represent a threat and must have been chosen because the predominantly Creole inhabitants had "no American ensign." Gerdes, "Reconnaissance Near Fort Morgan," 270.

9. According to George Riddell, the detained schooners were actually filled with wood that was destined to be delivered for the benefit of the Confederate military forces. The small vessels were even flying Confederate flags. But because the owners seemed to be poor men, and the cargoes of no direct military value, the blockaders simply seized the offending vessels' papers and flags and let them go. George Riddell to Brother John, Ship Island, May 19, 1862, Riddell Papers.

10. Named in honor of General Zebulon Pike, this fort was located overlooking the Rigolets, the nine-mile-long pass that connects Lake Pontchartrain north of New Orleans with Lake Borgne. The first construction on the triangular brick fort occurred between 1819 and 1827, with a second brick story added beginning in 1849. Although it was seized by the Confederates at the outset of the war, the Union regained possession of Fort Pike in early May 1862. Roberts, *Encyclopedia of Historic Forts*, 347.

11. A Union soldier described Ship Island as "the sandiest region this side of the Great Sahara," noting that on that island "the sand is of a dazzling white which glitters in the moonlight like snow, and by day dazzles and fatigues the eyes unless the weather be cloudy." John William De Forest, *A Volunteer's Adventures: A Union Captain's Record of the Civil War* (Baton Rouge: Louisiana State University Press, 1946), 3.

12. The name Rigolets (sometimes spelled Rigolettes) is generally believed to come from the French word "rigole," meaning trench or gutter.

13. F. H. Gerdes of the Coast Survey, who utilized *Sachem* extensively because of its shallow draft, reported that "within three miles of Gainesville, Mississippi, where the stream became extremely narrow and crooked, with the shores on both sides thickly wooded, the *Sachem* encountered a very sudden ambuscade, and received a heavy fire of musketry from the eastern bank. This was immediately returned from the vessel by some sixty rifle and musket shots, and discharges of small arms were continued in rapid succession from both sides for some time." Gerdes, "Reconnaissance Near Fort Morgan," 271.

14. One of the wounded was J. G. Oltmanns of the Coast Survey, who was severely injured in the left breast when *Sachem* was fired upon by Confederate riflemen on the shore. *Sachem* had gone up the Pearl River in an attempt to find some rebel steamers that were rumored to be up the river. After finding themselves in an ambush, *Sachem*'s crew returned fire, driving away the Confederates and actually shooting one of them down from a tree in which he was hiding. D. D. Porter to A. D. Bache, Ship Island, May 16, 1862, 18 ORN 395.

15. Named after a Pennsylvania creek that in turn derived its name from an Indian word meaning "running water," *Octorara* was a new double-ended side-wheel steamer that was commissioned in New York on February 28, 1862. DANFS, 5:137–138.

## Chapter 3

1. The composing stick and the rule were the printer's tools used in setting type.

2. At the time of the Civil War, Pensacola was the largest city in Florida. George F. Pearce, *Pensacola during the Civil War: A Thorn in the Side of the Confederacy* (Gainesville: University Press of Florida, 2000), 1. Because it had one of the finest harbors on the Gulf Coast, the U.S. Navy created a navy yard at Warrington, near the entrance to Pensacola Bay and about ten miles southwest of the city of Pensacola. To protect this important naval facility, a trio of forts (Barrancas, 1839–1845; Pickens, 1829–1834; and McRee, 1835–1839) had been erected at the entrance to the harbor. When Florida left the Union, the Confederates seized the Navy Yard and two of the forts that guarded it. But Fort Pickens, at the tip

of Santa Rosa Island, stayed in Union control, resisting several Confederate attempts to capture it. The Confederates were eventually forced to deploy their resources elsewhere, and on May 9, 1862, the retreating Confederate cavalry regiments set fire to the Navy Yard at Warrington, leaving it a ruin (still smoking) at the time of Gusley's visit three weeks later. Ibid., 2–26; Roberts, *Encyclopedia of Historic Forts*, 195–198; D. D. Porter to G. Welles, Pensacola, May 10, 1862, 18 ORN 478–479.

3. Although there is some conflict in the eyewitness accounts, Acting Quartermaster William Conway, a thirty-eight-year Navy veteran, is sometimes said to have hauled down the flag at the Pensacola Navy Yard when it was surrendered to the Confederates on January 12, 1861. Commodore James Armstrong, the sixty-six-year-old commandant of the Navy Yard, was later court-martialed for his conduct leading to this surrender. Pearce, *Pensacola during the Civil War*, 10–23; Ringle, *Life in Mr. Lincoln's Navy*, 140.

4. Problems at Pensacola were not confined to the Union sailors. At the end of 1861, when the town was still in Confederate hands, General Braxton Bragg encountered severe discipline problems with his troops in the area, most of which he blamed on the sale of intoxicating liquor in the town of Pensacola. He estimated that half his court-martials and all of his military executions resulted from drunkenness. When these problems became particularly severe, he (like Union officials later) issued orders prohibiting all soldiers and sailors from entering the town. Pearce, *Pensacola during the Civil War*, 99.

5. Not a word that is commonly used today, "indite" meant to set down or enter into writing. OED, 1419.

6. Near the end of May 1862, a false rumor swept through the Federal fleet that the Confederates were in the process of evacuating the forts at the entrance to Mobile Bay. Commander David Porter even reported to Navy officials in Washington, "I am under the impression that few men remain in [the Mobile forts], and that Fort Gaines is almost dismantled." D. D. Porter to G. Welles, Pensacola, May 30, 1862, 18 ORN 523.

## Chapter 4

1. Gusley is referring to the Union fleet's famous battle (described in Chapter 1) with these same forts in April 1862.

2. What Gusley called the U.S. Customhouse was actually the U.S. Mint, which had begun operations in New Orleans in 1838. A gambler named William Mumford tore down the U.S. flag that had been hoisted over the Mint by the Navy shortly after the city fell into Union hands. Special Order No. 10 was later issued by Benjamin Butler ordering that Mumford be executed for this offense. On June 7, 1862, the same day that Gusley arrived in New Orleans, the sentence was carried out. Although he was later criticized for overreacting to this incident, General Butler was satis-fied that his demonstration had served its purpose. As he said in his memoirs, "no scene approaching general disorder was ever afterwards witnessed during my time [in New Orleans.]" Butler, *Butler's Book*, 1:443.

3. This is a reference to Frances Trollope's book *Domestic Manners of the Americans*, which related incidents that took place during that British author's visit to America in 1827. During that visit, Mrs. Trollope was told wild stories, including a tale involving a crocodile that ate a man's wife and five children, which she dutifully recorded as fact. Frances Trollope, *Domestic Manners of the Americans* (1832; reprint, New York: Alfred A. Knopf, 1949), 21.

## Chapter 5

1. Artist Theodore R. Davis, who accompanied the Mortar Fleet on its voyage up the Mississippi, described Ellis' Cliff (or Ellis Bluff, as it was also sometimes known) as "probably the strongest position on the river below

Vicksburg," noting that at that place "the river seems surrounded on three sides by a towering cliff, from 250 to 300 feet in height." "Scenes on the Lower Mississippi," *Harper's Weekly* 6, no. 294 (August 16, 1862): 523.

2. The Confederate batteries at Ellis' Cliff were to pose a continuing problem for Federal transports heading up the Mississippi for Natchez. On the morning of June 25, this same rebel battery exchanged fire with *Kensington* and *Sarah Bruen*, wounding two members of their crews severely before the Union gunboats' heavier guns could find the enemy's range and silence the concealed battery. F. Crocker to D. Farragut, U.S.S. *Kensington*, June 27, 1862, 18 ORN 573–574.

3. Dogs were not the only pets on Union warships in the Gulf. Exotic pets were sometimes taken aboard because sailors believed that "if you want to tame anything, a wild beast for instance, or a woman, put them on board of a man of war." The same sailor on U.S.S. *Arizona* who made this comment noted that the frigate *Princeton* had a bear on board and claimed that the bear "was so tame that the Captain let him sign the ship's articles for three years." Letter from "Young Neptune," *(Toledo) Daily Commercial*, December 7, 1863.

4. Known as the "Queen City of the Bluff," Vicksburg was located atop three-hundred-foot bluffs along the Mississippi River about halfway between New Orleans and Memphis. President Lincoln told Commodore David Porter in early 1862 that as important as the capture of New Orleans had been to the Union war effort, the Confederacy could continue to successfully defy the North until Vicksburg, the "key" as Lincoln called it, was subdued. Dave Page, *Ships Versus Shore: Civil War Engagements along Southern Shores and Rivers* (Nashville: Rutledge Hill Press, 1994), 231–232.

5. Commander David Porter states in his report that on June 21, 1862, "I proceeded up toward the city of Vicksburg to obtain ranges and draw the fire of the enemy's forts, about which we had no information. The rebels allowed us to get within good range, when they opened on us from all their batteries, without, however, doing any harm, and

enabling us to get the desired information. I gave them four bombs to let them see they were in range and some 100-pound rifle shots, and returned to the anchorage, after satisfying myself about the proper position to place the mortar vessels in." Report of D. D. Porter, Vicksburg, July 3, 1862, 18 ORN 639.

6. Gusley's use of the term "contrabands" here to refer to escaped slaves is perhaps not as insulting as it might sound to the modern ear. Union abolitionist General Benjamin F. Butler first applied the term "contrabands" to fugitives at Fort Monroe in order to find a legal excuse not to return them to their owners. The Confiscation Act of August 1861 established the first official policy on slaves, providing that any fugitive slave used with his or her master's knowledge for the Confederate cause was to be officially considered a "contraband" and thus a prize of war who should be set free. Using these criteria, several commanders set up "contraband camps," like those mentioned by Gusley, where they provided to the best of their limited ability for the fugitives' welfare. Many were crowded into unhealthy camps where some died from disease, exposure, or, occasionally, starvation. One of these camps experienced a 25 percent mortality rate over a two-year period. Some of the refugees found these conditions so harsh that they returned voluntarily to their former owners. Faust, *Historical Times Encyclopedia of the Civil War*, 161–162 (entry on "Contrabands" by Patricia L. Faust).

7. In the letter read to Farragut's fleet, U.S. Navy Secretary Gideon Welles wrote: "Our Navy, fruitful with victories, presents no more signal achievement than this, nor is there an exploit surpassing it recorded in the annals of naval warfare ... [Y]ourself, your officers, and our brave sailors and marines, whose courage and daring bear historic renown, have now a nation's gratitude and applause." G. Welles to D. G. Farragut, Navy Department, May 10, 1862, 18 ORN 246.

8. The phrase "infernal machines" was used by the Union Navy to refer to unconventional weapons like mines and torpedoes and would eventually be extended to include submarines and torpedo boats.

9. "Secesh" is a shortened form of the word "Secessionist" and was a derisive term commonly used by Northerners for the Confederacy and its rebellious inhabitants.

10. Commander Porter reported that "the enemy opened on [the Mortar Flotilla] from all their batteries in range, but though they fired all around and over them, none were struck. A kind Providence seems to look after this little fleet." Report of D. D. Porter, Vicksburg, July 3, 1862, 18 ORN 639.

11. Although Gusley is correct in his observation that none of the batteries was "silenced" or stopped from firing for any sustained period, Commodore Farragut (certainly no fan of mortars) reported after the battle that "The Mortar Flotilla have never done better service than at Vicksburg, notwithstanding the imperfection of their fuzes. I have no doubt that they did the forts on the heights great damage, and on the morning of the attack did much to distract the fire from the fleet." D. Farragut to G. Welles, Above Vicksburg, June 30, 1862, 18 ORN 591.

12. The steamers *Brooklyn*, *Kennebec*, and *Katahdin* did not get past the Confederate batteries. Captain Thomas Craven, in command of the *Brooklyn*, was later sent home to the North because of this failure. D. Farragut to T. T. Craven, Above Vicksburg, July 1, 1862, 18 ORN 605.

13. The steamer *John P. Jackson* "was struck badly with rifle shell, one of which exploded in her wheelhouse, disabling the man at the wheel by cutting off his leg, and knocking her steering apparatus to pieces." When *Clifton* tried to come to *Jackson*'s rescue, a 7-inch shot went through *Clifton*'s boiler. Commander Porter reported that "by this catastrophe six of the men in the magazine were scalded to death; others were scalded severely. The steam drove eight or ten men overboard, one of whom was drowned." Report of D. D. Porter, Vicksburg, July 3, 1862, 18 ORN 640–641. During this fight, the steam and hot water from *Clifton*'s ruptured boiler rushed out and filled the berth deck. According to one of *Clifton*'s officers, "It was an hour before we could go down to the berth deck and learn the full extent of the disaster. On doing so, we found six men scalded to death, presenting the most horrid spectacle I ever witnessed." John R. Bartlett, *Memoirs of Rhode Island Officers Who Were Engaged in the Service of Their Country During the Great Rebellion of the South* (Providence: Sidney S. Rider & Brother, 1867), 298 (statement of Robert Rhodes).

14. Commander Porter reported that "after the woods were well shelled the pickets went in and captured three rebel soldiers, who were helplessly stuck in the mud from which they had difficulty in extricating themselves, and cried out lustily that they had surrendered. They were brought in with their arms and accouterments. . . . In going over the ground afterwards our men found evidence of a general stampede throughout the woods. Amongst other things they picked up from the mud were the heavy boots of a general officer with silver spurs on." Report of D. D. Porter, Vicksburg, July 3, 1862, 18 ORN 642.

15. The Confederate surprise attack on the mortar vessels from the swampy woods lining the river had made Porter concerned that another such attack might be attempted. To prepare for this possibility, Gusley and a party of forty-nine other marines were landed to serve as pickets. At Porter's direction, the Union shore party also had "a large bell slung up in the woods with lines leading to it from different points so that the pickets might give immediate alarm, after which the Mortar Flotilla went to their repose with great confidence." Ibid.

16. On November 25, 1778, British forces demanded the immediate surrender of Fort Morris in Liberty County, Georgia. Colonel John McIntosh, in command of the American garrison defending it, replied with the famous words, "Come and take it." Roberts, *Encyclopedia of American Forts*, 230. This would also later be the official motto of Texas rebels at the Battle of Gonzales (October 2, 1835).

17. During the entirety of 1862, the Confederate battery at Grand Gulf was a continuing thorn in the side to passing Union ships. On several occasions (the most recent only about two weeks before Gusley passed by Grand Gulf), Union gunboats exchanged fire with the

battery, causing substantial damage to the city and the lower battery but leaving the gun positions on top of the bluff largely intact. T. T. Craven to wife, New Orleans, June 3, 1862, 18 ORN 534–535; G. H. Preble to H. H. Bell, Below Vicksburg, July 10, 1862, 18 ORN 673; D. G. Farragut to G. Welles, Baton Rouge, June 16, 1862. 18 ORN 561.

18. The "rebel ram" that Gusley describes was the C.S.S. *Arkansas*, which turned out to be the most successful Confederate ironclad to ever enter the Mississippi. On July 15, 1862, *Arkansas* entered the Mississippi River and steamed slowly through the Union fleet above Vicksburg, doing significant damage to a number of the Federal ships it passed on its way down to Vicksburg. On the night of July 15 Farragut took his fleet downstream past the city, firing at the Confederate ironclad in an unsuccessful attempt to destroy the vessel. It was this action at dusk in which Gusley and the Mortar Flotilla joined.

Faust, *Historical Encyclopedia of the Civil War*, 22–23 (entry on "Arkansas, C.S.S.," by William N. Still Jr.).

19. On the morning of July 15, the mortar schooner *Sidney C. Jones* went aground below Vicksburg. The commander of the Mortar Flotilla became concerned about its capture when he learned that the Confederate ironclad *Arkansas* was steaming through the fleet up the river and ordered that preparations be made to blow the schooner up if it became necessary. The order was misunderstood, and the schooner was blown up prematurely. W. B. Renshaw to G. Welles, Mississippi River, July 23, 1862, 19 ORN 29.

20. Davis had replaced Admiral Andrew H. Foote in command of the Western Gunboat Flotilla on the Mississippi River in May 1862. Heidler and Heidler, *Encyclopedia of the American Civil War*, 2:560–561 (entry on "Davis, Charles Henry," by David S. Heidler and Jeanne T. Heidler).

## Chapter 6

1. Union naval forces seized control of Baton Rouge without resistance on May 9, 1862. J. S. Palmer to B. F. Bryan, Baton Rouge, May 9, 1862, 18 ORN 474–475. But on August 5, 1862, Confederate forces attempted to recapture the city, an attempt that was thwarted only by covering shellfire from Union naval vessels moored at the city's docks. The battle for the city was essentially a stalemate, but the Union eventually retained control. William A. Spedale, *The Battle of Baton Rouge: 1862* (Baton Rouge: Land and Land Publishing, 1985), 33–39.

2. The account of the battle that Gusley received was confused and erroneous. In charge of the Confederate force was General John C. Breckinridge, who had with him a force of about 2,600 men. General Thomas Williams had about the same number of Union defenders. At dawn on August 5, 1862, in a dense fog, the Confederate land troops attacked, eventually flanking the Union right and leading to a disorderly retreat back through town toward the river. The Confederate battle plan called for C.S.S. *Arkansas* to support the at-

tack by dispersing the Union gunboats. But the rebel ironclad had developed engine trouble north of the city, leading to its absence and eventually to its destruction. The Union gunboats provided protection to the fleeing Federals, and Breckinridge was forced to call off his attack by about 10 A.M. Union casualties were about 400, with General Williams being one of those killed. Confederate casualties were about 450. Heidler and Heidler, *Encyclopedia of the American Civil War*, 1:190–191 (entry on "Baton Rouge, Battle of," by James V. Holton); Richard N. Current, ed., *Encyclopedia of the Confederacy* (New York: Simon & Schuster, 1993), 1:140–141 (entry on "Baton Rouge, Louisiana," by Mark Carleton).

3. Despite the report that Gusley received, the Fourth Wisconsin infantry regiment was actually used primarily as a reserve force and did not play a particularly prominent part in the battle.

4. This erroneous report, which circulated very soon after the battle, apparently originated from the capture of the severely wounded Confederate General Charles Clark. Report of

T. W. Cahill, Baton Rouge, August 5, 1862, 15 OR 54; T. W. Cahill to J. C. Breckinridge, Baton Rouge, August 6, 1862, 15 OR 55.

5. On August 9, 1862, a Federal fleet under the command of Flag-Officer Farragut appeared off of the town of Donaldsonville and proceeded to destroy a large portion of it in accordance with the warning *Westfield* had brought. As Farragut reported to Washington, "I burned down the hotels and wharf buildings, also the dwelling houses and other buildings of a Mr. Phillippe Landry, who is said to be a captain of guerillas. He fired upon our men, but they chased him off. We also brought off some ten or twelve of his negroes and supplied ourselves with cattle and sheep from his place." D. G. Farragut

to G. Welles, New Orleans, August 10, 1862, 19 ORN 141. Although, as Gusley relates, most of the structures along the riverfront in Donaldsonville were destroyed, certain structures like the Catholic Church and the associated convent and orphanage were spared. William A. Spedale, *Fort Butler, 1863: Donaldsonville, Louisiana* (Baton Rouge: W. A. Spedale, 1997), 5–7.

6. Farragut's destruction of most of Donaldsonville appears to have had its intended effect on residents in some other Louisiana towns. Two days after the bombardment, resolutions were formally adopted in Ascension and St. James Parishes ordering a cessation to any and all hostile acts against Union shipping. Spedale, *Fort Butler*, 9.

## Chapter 7

1. Lemons were apparently very popular at Pensacola. One visiting Union sailor recorded the treat of enjoying a cool drink made from shaved ice and fruit syrup. He noted that lemons were the only fruit allowed on Santa Rosa Island. Acting under the authority of martial law, the provost marshal had forbidden the importation of any other fruit, fearing that the sailors would overindulge in such delicacies and make themselves sick. Cruise of the U.S. Gunboat *Cayuga*, entry for June 26, 1862, Samuel B. Massa Papers, Special Collections Research Center, E. S. Bird Library, Syracuse University, Syracuse, New York.

2. That Gusley's supposedly revised and updated information on the Battle of Baton Rouge is still grossly erroneous more than a month following the battle shows just how difficult it was to obtain accurate and contemporaneous wartime news, particularly in the Navy.

3. Farragut was the most senior of four officers in active service who were made rear admirals effective July 16, 1862. Thompson, *Civil War Commodores and Admirals*, 59–61.

4. Van Buren died at Kinderhook, New York, on July 24, 1862. At the direction of President Abraham Lincoln, the Secretary of the Navy issued instructions that "thirty minute guns,

commencing at noon, be fired, on the day after the receipt of this General Order, at the Navy Yards, Naval Stations and on board the vessels of the Navy in commission; that their flags be displayed at half mast for one week, and that crepe be worn on the left arm by all officers of the Navy for a period of six months." General Order of Secretary of the Navy Gideon Welles, July 25, 1862.

5. Wilson's Zouaves, also known as Billy Wilson's Zouaves, was another name for the Sixth New York Infantry Regiment, which was organized in New York City. It spent the first two years of the war in Florida, mainly on Santa Rosa Island near Pensacola. The regiment had a poor reputation. One army regular recalled that Wilson himself was merely a "Tammany [ward] healer from the slums of New York, and his entire regiment was composed of the same character. His regiment had been selected especially for its noted worthless character, and [was] sent to Santa Rosa as a place where it could do the least harm." Pearce, *Pensacola during the Civil War*, 107.

6. Baton Rouge was indeed abandoned by the Federals on August 21, 1862, but on December 17, 1862, they returned with a larger force, which regained and occupied the city for the rest of the war. Current, *Encyclopedia of the*

*Confederacy*, 1:140–141 (entry on "Baton Rouge, Louisiana," by Mark Carleton).

7. Gusley and the other men in the naval service were the beneficiaries of a mail service that was far superior to the postal service enjoyed by their land counterparts. Some of the large supply steamers, like the two mentioned here, could carry as many as four hundred thousand letters and two thousand parcels to men serving in the blockading squadrons. Ringle, *Life in Mr. Lincoln's Navy*, 83.

8. It is likely that Gusley is referring to the comet Swift-Tuttle (sometimes referred to as "the war comet"), which was discovered in 1862. However, it is also possible that he is referring to the Perseid meteor shower, which makes its appearance every year in the middle of August. The Perseid shower results from debris associated with comet Swift-Tuttle.

9. In a joint resolution approved July 11, 1862, Congress officially thanked Farragut and all the men who served under him "for their successful operations on the Mississippi River, and for their gallantry displayed in the capture of Forts Jackson and St. Philip, and the city of New Orleans, and in the destruction of the enemy's gunboats and armed flotilla." 18 ORN 248.

10. In an act approved July 14, 1862, Congress proclaimed that "the spirit ration in the United States shall forever cease" and provided that "no spirituous liquors shall be admitted on board vessels of war, except as medical stores." To (in theory at least) compensate the sailors for this change, Congress raised their pay five cents per day. General Order, Navy Department, July 17, 1862, 7 ORN 584; *Civil War Naval Chronology: 1861–1865* (Washington: Naval

History Division of the Navy Department, 1971), 2:81.

11. A "gill" was a measure of liquid equivalent to one-quarter of a pint. OED, 1142.

12. The equinoxial (sometimes spelled "equinoctial") storm was the gale that was expected to take place at approximately the same time as the autumn equinox, when the period of daylight and darkness was exactly the same. OED, 887.

13. A character in Charles Dickens' *David Copperfield*, Wilkins Micawber was an impractical optimist who was always waiting for "something to turn up."

14. Construction of a brick fort on Ship Island had begun in 1856 but was still incomplete when the Civil War broke out in 1861. The Confederates seized the fort and named it Fort Twiggs after General David E. Twiggs. When the Confederates abandoned Ship Island in the fall of 1861, the uncompleted fort was occupied by Union troops. They soon began construction of a large brick fortification. That fort was eventually named Fort Massachusetts, probably in honor of the Union ship by that same name that had shelled the original site of the fort early in the war. Roberts, *Encyclopedia of Historic Forts*, 446–447.

15. This was Robert E. Lee's first campaign to invade Union territory, which culminated in the Battle of Antietam (Sharpsburg) on September 17, 1862.

16. Not a commonly used word today, "descant" means to comment or discourse about a subject. OED, 696.

17. John Godfrey Saxe (1816–1887) was a lawyer from Vermont who wrote popular poetry, most of which consisted of short, humorous pieces like this one that were published in magazines like *Harper's Weekly* or *Atlantic Monthly*.

## Chapter 8

1. With the best port on the Texas coast, Galveston was the second largest city in the state in 1862. The Union had been blockading the port since July 1861 and had been threatening to capture it since at least May 1862. Edward T. Cotham, Jr., *Battle on the Bay: The Civil*

*War Struggle for Galveston* (Austin: University of Texas Press, 1998), 1–2, 52–55.

2. Located at the border between Texas and Louisiana, Sabine Pass is the tidal outlet into the Gulf of Mexico for Sabine Lake, which is formed by the confluence of the Sabine and Neches Rivers.

3. In this Confederate fort were Richard "Dick" Dowling and the Davis Guard (Company F of Cook's First Texas Heavy Artillery), who, after firing a token shot, retreated from the fort in accordance with long-standing orders. Cotham, *Battle on the Bay*, 62.

4. "Quaker guns" were logs that had been cut and painted to resemble cannons from a distance. The Confederates at Galveston had become quite adept at producing these artificial artillery pieces in great quantities.

5. Commodore Renshaw on board U.S.S. *Westfield* (his flag ship) threatened that he would either "hoist the United States flag over the city of Galveston or its ashes." P. O. Hebert to J. Deshler, San Antonio, October 15, 1862, 15 OR 147.

6. The term "traps" was a shortened version of the word "trappings" that referred to the usual or official dress and portable possessions of a person. OED, 3387.

7. Pelican Spit (today part of Pelican Island) was a small sandbar or island near the entrance to Galveston Harbor.

8. The "Custom-house" to which Gusley refers was the combined customhouse, courthouse, and post office built by the U.S. government in Galveston in 1861. Its ironwork had been constructed under the supervision of Major Robert Anderson (who would surrender Fort Sumter at the outset of the war). Onsite construction was supervised by Walter H. Stevens, who would later become chief engineer for Robert E. Lee's Army of Northern Virginia. Donald J. Lehman, *Lucky Landmark: A Study of a Design and Its Survival* (Washington, D.C.: General Services Administration Public Buildings Service, 1973), 33–35.

9. The son of a Protestant Episcopal bishop by the same name, Jonathan Wainwright was born in New York City in 1821. As commander of *Harriet Lane*, Wainwright participated in the Union fleet's actions at New Orleans and Vicksburg. His grandson gained fame during World War II as the American general who defended and ultimately was forced to surrender Bataan and Corregidor.

10. Originally the place where the ferry left for Galveston, Virginia Point was at the mainland end of the railroad bridge to Galveston Island that was completed in 1860. Ron Tyler, ed., *New Handbook of Texas* (Austin: Texas State Historical Association, 1996), 6:760 (entry on "Virginia Point" by Priscilla Myers Benham). At Virginia Point, the Confederates built Fort Hebert, one of the largest fortifications in the vicinity.

11. "The Girl [Gal] I Left Behind Me" was a popular song at the time of the Civil War. The song lyrics are usually attributed to a poem written by Samuel Lover in the 1750s.

## Chapter 9

1. *Proverbs*, 27:1.

2. Originally called Espíritu Santo and later referred to as Costa y Bahia de San Bernardo, Matagorda Bay is one of the largest bays along the Texas Gulf Coast. Protected by the Matagorda Peninsula, the cities along the bay were active ports of call for blockade runners. Tyler, *New Handbook of Texas*, 4:555–556 (entries on "Matagorda, Texas," by Diana J. Kleiner and "Matagorda Bay" by Art Leatherwood).

3. According to the *Atlas to Accompany the Official Records of the Union and Confederate Armies* (Washington, D.C.: Government Printing Office, 1891), hereinafter ORA, Union maps actually recognized four subdivisions within Matagorda Bay—Lavaca Bay, Tres Palacios Bay, Matagorda Bay, and Powderhorn Bay. ORA Plate 157.

4. *Westfield* ran aground so frequently during its armed reconnaissance of the Texas Coast that a joke made the rounds of the Union fleet that Commodore Renshaw only kept *Clifton* around so that it would be available to tug *Westfield* off the sandbars on which it seemed to end up at least once a day. A. J. H. Duganne, *Camps and Prisons: Twenty Months in the Department of the Gulf* (New York: J. P. Robens, 1865), 233.

5. This secessionist reception is not surprising. The citizens of Matagorda County had voted for secession in 1861 by the commanding margin of 243 to 8,

and the residents of Calhoun County, on the other side of the bay, voted for secession 276 to 16. Ernest W. Winkler, ed., *Journal of the Secession Convention of Texas, 1861* (Austin: Austin Printing Co., 1912), 89.

6. Not a word in common usage today, "descried" is the past tense of the verb "descry," meaning to get sight of, discover, or observe. OED, 697.

7. A nine-inch Dahlgren gun, like the one that *Westfield* employed here, weighed about 9,000 pounds and had an effective range of about 2,100 yards. Angus Konstam, *Mississippi River Gunboats of the American Civil War, 1861–65* (Oxford, England: Osprey Publishing, 2002), 20.

8. Captured in Matagorda Bay in October, the schooner *Lecompte* would stay in Union hands only until January 1, 1863, when it was recaptured by the Confederates at the Battle of Galveston. In May 1865, the ship ran aground on Bird Key in Galveston Bay, where it ultimately became an abandoned wreck. Paul H. Silverstone, *Civil War Navies, 1855–1883* (Annapolis, Maryland: Naval Institute Press, 2001), 176–177.

9. Spanish for "thick brush," Matagorda was one of the earliest settlements established by Steven F. Austin along the Texas Gulf Coast. Built where the Colorado River emptied into Matagorda Bay, Matagorda was a fairly sophisticated town that by the late 1830s possessed a newspaper, a hotel, and a theater. It was an important home port for Texas blockade runners. Tyler, *New Handbook of Texas*, 4:555 (entry on "Matagorda, Texas," by Diana J. Kleiner).

10. Established where Powderhorn Lake connects with Matagorda Bay, this town (a southern extension of Indianola) was strategically located along the transshipment route between Matagorda Bay and the river system that led to San Antonio. Tyler, *New Handbook of Texas*, 5:304 (entry on "Powder Horn, Texas," anonymous). By the time of the Civil War, Indianola was the second most prominent port in Texas. In 1856 Indianola was the subject of a bizarre experiment in which the army landed two shipments of camels to determine if they would be a reliable source of transportation for military

supplies. Ibid., 3:830 (entry on "Indianola, Texas," by Brownson Malsch).

11. As the conversation was reported by these "city fathers," Commodore Renshaw said that he had come to take possession of all the cities on Matagorda Bay. Although he admitted that he did not at that time have enough U.S. Army troops to garrison these towns, he intended to come ashore to buy provisions. If his men were interfered with in any way during the course of this task, the commodore warned, he would not hesitate to fire on the towns. Commodore Renshaw "hoped such a collision would not occur" but said that he must have beef, "and if he could buy and pay for it he would do so; if not, he would take it by some means and at some place." H. B. Cleveland to D. D. Shea, Indianola, October 26, 1862, 19 ORN 794–795.

12. Although there was a San Antonio newspaper called the *Herald*, Gusley is in all probability referring to James Gordon Bennett's controversial and popular publication, the *New York Herald*.

13. Confirming Gusley's account, an officer aboard *Clifton* reported that on October 26, "we sent a boat ashore and demanded the surrender of [Indianola], which they complied with immediately as they had no guns to defend it." Bartlett, *Memoirs of Rhode Island Officers*, 299 (statement of Robert Rhodes).

14. Matagorda was built where the Colorado River emptied into Matagorda Bay. However, the Colorado was a muddy river that deposited its sediment into the bay over such a wide area that only small boats could approach within four miles of the town. Brownson Malsch, *Indianola: The Mother of Western Texas* (Austin: State House Press, 1988), 2.

15. Meaning "the cow" in Spanish, Lavaca was situated on a bluff about fifteen feet above the western coast of Lavaca Bay. Today called Port Lavaca, it is the seat of Calhoun County. At the time of the Civil War it had a population of just over five hundred, about half that of nearby Indianola. Tyler, *New Handbook of Texas*, 5:281 (entry on "Port Lavaca, Texas," by Lonnie F. Maywald).

16. The Confederates reported

later that they had only been given an hour and a half to remove the women, children, and sick people from town. Originally limited to one hour, this evacuation period was extended by thirty minutes because yellow fever was raging in the town. G. E. Conklin to E. F. Gray, Lavaca, November 1, 1862, 19 ORN 800–801.

17. At first, the Union ships fired without receiving any reply from the Confederate guns. That soon changed. As Robert Rhodes on *Clifton* recorded, "We had been shelling the town and batteries for some time, and had not received a single shot from them. We could not see a single man about the batteries, but we could see a large secesh flag flying between the two batteries. As they did not open fire at us, we moved up within about half a mile of the town, when all of a sudden the batteries opened fire upon us, the shot and shell striking all around, but none of them happened to hit either of us; but to speak the truth they quite surprised us all. We soon backed out of their range, and kept up a heavy fire upon them until dark, when we ceased firing and anchored for the night." Bartlett, *Memoirs of the Rhode Island Officers*, 300 (statement of Robert Rhodes). A reporter from Lavaca described the Union bombardment of the town as a "murderous fire of shell and shot," noting that it was a miracle that none of the city's women and children were killed or wounded. "The Bombardment of Lavaca," *(Houston) Tri-Weekly Telegraph*, November 10, 1862.

18. The Parrott gun, which weighed about 9,700 pounds, was a rifled iron artillery piece that was distinguished by its single reinforcing band, placed on the gun while the barrel was rotated with cooling water sprayed inside. Developed by Robert Parker Parrott, the gun was one of the most widely used rifled guns of the Civil War. Its critics contended, as *Westfield*'s experience supports, that these heavier rifles tended to burst after sustained use. Faust, *Historical Times Encyclopedia of the Civil War*, 558 (entry on "Parrott

gun" by Les D. Jensen); Jack Coggins, *Arms and Equipment of the Civil War* (Wilmington, North Carolina: Broadfoot Publishing, 1962), 144.

19. Gusley was probably right. On December 24, 1864, during the bombardment of Fort Fisher, a similar Parrott rifle exploded on board U.S.S. *Ticonderoga*. That explosion killed eight men and wounded twelve more. C. Steedman to D. Porter, Off Beaufort, North Carolina, December 30, 1864, 11 ORN 328. The explosion of another gun of the same type on board *Juniata* during the same bombardment killed five men and wounded eight more. A. C. Gorgas to W. R. Taylor, Off Wilmington, North Carolina, December 24, 1864, 11 ORN 322.

20. On the morning of November 1, 1862, the Confederates did not return fire in response to the renewed Union bombardment. A Union officer reported, "Our shells did a great deal of damage to the town. We could see them strike the houses, bursting and throwing the boards, clapboards and shingles in every direction." Bartlett, *Memoirs of the Rhode Island Officers*, 300 (statement of Robert Rhodes). The Confederates reported that during the two days of fighting the Union fleet had fired at Lavaca in all "252 shots and shell, 174 the first day and 78 the second, nearly all of them from 32 and 64 pounder rifled guns." G. E. Conklin to E. F. Gray, Lavaca, November 1, 1862, 19 ORN 801. One result of the Battle of Port Lavaca was that local resident Edgar Collins Singer was inspired to design a series of ingenious mines and torpedoes for the Confederacy. He would also play an important role in the design and construction of the Confederate submarine *Hunley*. Mark K. Ragan, *Submarine Warfare in the Civil War* (Cambridge, Massachusetts: Da Capo Press, 2002), 111–117.

21. *Owasco* was one of the ninety-day gunboats, so called because they had been constructed in that short period of time in order to meet the urgent demands of the U.S. Navy. Silverstone, *Civil War Navies*, 30–31.

*Chapter 10*

1. Seven men went ashore on Bolivar Point at 6:15 A.M. About an hour later, volleys of musketry were heard coming from the shore. *Owasco* replied by firing its rifled gun into the bushes near where the boat had landed. A launch was sent to retrieve what was left of the landing party but returned with only one of the boat's crew (John Heath). A short time later another wounded man (William Senelet) was paroled and returned to the fleet. Abstract log of *Owasco* (prepared by John G. Arbona), November 14, 1862, 19 ORN 345.

2. Commodore William B. Renshaw, in command of the Union fleet at Galveston, informed his superiors that the deserters he was receiving were "flying from the terrors of the conscription" and stated, "I am of the opinion that we have at last captured a place with strong Union proclivities among the lower and middle classes." W. B. Renshaw to D. G. Farragut, Galveston, October 8, 1862, 19 ORN 258.

3. Hickley, who represented himself to be the "Commander and Senior Naval Officer at Nassau," made a practice of regularly patrolling the Southern coast to assert the rights of British ships and sailors caught up in the Union blockade. H. D. Hickley to G. Gansevoort, Nassau, July 25, 1862, 1 ORN 410.

4. "Bolivar channel," as Gusley refers to it, is today called Bolivar Roads and is the channel between the tip of Galveston Island and Bolivar Peninsula. This channel leads from the Gulf of Mexico into Galveston Bay. Tyler, *New Handbook of Texas*, 1:627 (entry on "Bolivar Roads," anonymous).

5. When the Civil War erupted, there was not a national Thanksgiving holiday as there is today. Instead, as Gusley notes, the governors of some states, particularly the New England states, declared such a holiday as a matter of local custom. The first national Thanksgiving holiday to be declared by the U.S. government since 1815 occurred in 1862 when President Lincoln declared a Thanksgiving holiday for Sunday, April 13, following the Union victory at Shiloh. On October 3, 1863, Lincoln declared a national day of Thanksgiving that year for the last Thursday in November. This Thanksgiving date, the first of the war that was general in nature and not tied to a specific battle or event, became the first of the national holidays that Americans celebrate today.

6. A "holystone" was a piece of sandstone used by sailors to scour the deck of a ship. Some sources say that the name originated because a sailor had to get down on his knees in a prayerlike posture to use it. OED, 1321. Other sources suggest that the name "holystone" originated when English sailors obtained small pieces of a broken church monument to use in scrubbing their ships' decks. Ringle, *Life in Mr. Lincoln's Navy*, 45.

7. Gusley's report of this incident emphasizes again the danger of relying on rumors spread among sailors as to occurrences on shore. What actually happened in Galveston on the evening of December 1 was that an inebriated one-armed man named Tom Barnett had told a Union sentry to "Go to Hell!" and fired a shotgun once before running for safety. The brief exchange of fire produced no casualties. Cotham, *Battle on the Bay*, 70–71.

8. *Tennessee* was a side-wheel steamboat built in Baltimore in 1854. Used first as a Confederate blockade runner, it was captured by the Union fleet as part of the operations leading to the capture of New Orleans. It was officially added to the U.S. Navy in May 1862. Because of its speed, this vessel (eventually renamed *Mobile*) was used frequently to chase blockade runners. It also saw frequent service as a dispatch boat. DANFS, 4:400–401, 7:86.

9. When Commodore Renshaw passed these rumors along to Admiral Farragut, the admiral responded angrily, inquiring, "Has it come to this, that four gunboats, armed with 8, 9, and 11 inch guns, are to be driven out of a harbor by the report of some 'reliable person' that preparations are making to drive them out of the harbor?" D. G. Farragut to W. B. Renshaw, New Orleans, December 12, 1862, 19 ORN 404.

10. Acting Master Quincy Hooper reported to his superior in Galveston,

"I have received positive information that the vessels under my command are to be attacked immediately by a strong rebel force, consisting of three steamers, aided by a land force with two heavy guns." Report of Q. A. Hooper, Sabine Pass, December 5, 1862, 19 ORN 392. Such an attack by cottonclad steamers did eventually take place at Sabine Pass, but not until January 21, 1863.

11. The Confederates had built a small fort at Eagle Grove, the point where the railroad bridge from the mainland reached Galveston Island. They built a larger fortification, Fort Hebert, on Virginia Point near the mainland end of the railroad bridge to Galveston Island.

12. Designed originally by John Dahlgren, these guns were shaped like a soda bottle, with most of their weight and reinforcement at the breech. The nine-inch model taken on board *Westfield* was one of the most common broadside carriage-mounted guns used by the Navy. Heidler and Heidler, *Encyclopedia of the American Civil War*, 2:547–548 (entry on "Dahlgren Guns" by James H. Meredith).

13. There was a condition placed on this free transportation offer. As Galveston's best history of the period records: "[The refugees] received notification that they must take the oath of allegiance, and all those who refused would have to return to their homes in the city; that those who took the oath would be taken to New Orleans, and there, if they desired, they could join the [Union] Texas Brigade, then being raised in that city by Judge E. J. Davis. . . . The most of them took the oath, and were transported to New Orleans; and those who did not were compelled to return to their homes." Charles W. Hayes, *Galveston: A History of the Island and the City* (typeset 1879; printed, Austin: Jenkins Garrett Press, 1974), 1:543–544.

14. These civilians, who had until this time lived on a wharf guarded continually by a steamer, had become increasingly problematic to Commodore Renshaw, and he complained of "the difficulty of protecting them in case of an attack, and the certainty that I would soon have to feed them." Renshaw noted that he could not simply send them away because "some of the men have had prices placed upon their heads and all of them are obnoxious to the enemy." W. B. Renshaw to D. G. Farragut, Galveston, December 15, 1862, 19 ORN 431.

15. This is the same gun (depicted by Dr. Nestell in Figure 83) that had been spiked and abandoned by Dick Dowling and the Davis Guard when the Union fleet first entered Galveston Bay in October 1862.

16. Shindy, sometimes also called shinty, was a game like hockey, so named because the players were likely to receive blows on their shins from the sticks with which it was played.

17. This is the second line of a later (seldom-heard) verse of the song "Jingle Bells," which probably was itself taken from an earlier song, also called "Go It While You're Young," that apparently originated in the wake of the financial panic of 1857.

18. Less than a month later *Rachel Seaman* would be ordered to the navy yard for repairs based on the representations of her captain that she was leaking so badly as to destroy her ammunition and injure the health of her crew. H. H. Bell to Q. A. Hooper, Galveston, January 18, 1863, 19 ORN 539.

19. On December 24, 1862, three companies of the Forty-second Massachusetts Infantry Regiment arrived in Galveston under the command of Colonel Isaac Burrell. These troops, actually less than three hundred men, were placed ashore the next day, where they occupied a position at the end of Kuhn's Wharf. They fortified this position pending the expected arrival of the rest of their regiment. Because the Confederates recaptured Galveston on January 1, 1863, no reinforcements would arrive in time. Report of I. S. Burrell, Galveston, December 29, 1862, 15 OR 204–205; Cotham, *Battle on the Bay*, 73–86.

20. Although money had been appropriated for a lighthouse at Galveston as early as 1847, title complications delayed its construction until 1852. On Christmas Day 1852, construction of the sixty-five-foot iron tower and an adjacent wooden keeper's dwelling was completed. In 1857 the height of the tower was raised by twenty-four feet, and a

year later a new, more powerful lens was installed. When the Civil War began, the Confederates ceased operating this light, fearing that it would be a navigational aid to the blockading Union fleet. As Gusley observed, the light was destroyed just before the Battle of Galveston, and the Confederates took the ironwork off to be used in military projects. After the war, the lighthouse engineer found nothing left of the lighthouse except its concrete base. T. Lindsay Baker, *Lighthouses of Texas* (College Station: Texas A&M Press, 1991), 57–59; David L. Cipra, *Lighthouses, Lightships, and the Gulf of Mexico* (Alexandria, Virginia: Cypress Communications, 1997), 177–179.

21. On January 1, 1863, the Confederates under General John Bankhead Magruder recaptured Galveston in one of the most unusual battles of the Civil War. At about 5 A.M., rebel artillery opened fire on the Federal fleet from all along the waterfront. As the Union gunboats were dealing with this threat, two cottonclad steamers approached from the rear and rammed the steamer *Harriet Lane*, seizing the most powerful gunboat and threatening to turn it against the rest of the Union fleet. Gusley's ship, *Westfield*, ran aground earlier in the evening on Pelican Spit. In the process of blowing up *Westfield* to keep it out of the hands of the enemy, Commodore Renshaw made a catastrophic mistake and triggered a premature explosion that killed him and a number of *Westfield*'s crew. Cotham, *Battle on the Bay*, 113–139.

22. Gusley was formally added to *Clifton*'s Marine Guard effective January 15, 1863.

## Chapter 11

1. The phrase "Simon pure" means the genuine person or thing. It had its origin in a character named Simon Pure, a Quaker who was impersonated by another character in the comedy "A Bold Stroke for a Wife" written in 1717 by Susannah Centlivre, an English dramatist and actress. In that play, a Colonel Feignwell passes himself off for Simon Pure and wins the heart of the leading lady. But while attempting to secure the approval of her guardian, Simon Pure himself arrives and proves beyond a doubt that he is the one true Simon Pure. E. Cobham Brewer, *The Dictionary of Phrase and Fable* (Philadelphia: Henry Altemus, 1898), 1143–1144.

2. *Hatteras* was a 210-foot-long sidewheel steamer that was purchased by the Navy in September 1861. It served with distinction off the Florida coast, not only maintaining the blockade but capturing a small shore garrison at Cedar Keys harbor. It was transferred to the West Blockading Squadron shortly before its capture off Galveston in January 1863. *DANFS*, 3:270–271.

3. On the afternoon of January 11, 1863, the Union steamer *Hatteras* was sent in chase of an unknown vessel off the coast of Galveston. After luring *Hatteras* more than ten miles from the rest of the blockading fleet, the strange ship turned on the Union steamer and attacked, proving to be the Confederate commerce raider C.S.S. *Alabama* (also known as the "290" because of its hull number in the English shipyard where it was built). In a battle lasting less than fifteen minutes, *Hatteras* was sunk. Contrary to Gusley's information, the sinking ship's crew was taken aboard *Alabama* and was later released in Jamaica. Faust, *Historical Times Illustrated Encyclopedia of the Civil War*, 3–4, 350 (entries on "Alabama, C.S.S.," by William N. Still Jr. and on "Hatteras, U.S.S.," by Norman C. Delaney).

4. Farragut wrote to a friend that he had been forced to send *Clifton* up the Mississippi River for the time being because her officers and crew were "so convinced that she will founder at sea that they are deserting and completely demoralized." D. G. Farragut to J. Alden, New Orleans, January 17, 1863, 19 ORN 536.

5. Brigadier General Cuvier Grover reached Baton Rouge on December 17, 1862, with 4,500 Union soldiers. Faced with this force, the Confederates evacuated the city without a fight. Report of C. Grover, Baton Rouge, December 17, 1862, 15 OR 191–192.

## Chapter 12

1. The Second Regiment of Louisiana Native Guards was one of the first black regiments to see action in the Civil War. On January 12, 1863, Colonel Nathan Daniels and seven companies of the Guards arrived in Ship Island, joining the Thirteenth Maine, a white regiment. On January 26, at a joint battalion drill, the white officers of the Maine regiment refused to follow the orders of black officers who were superior in rank. Colonel Daniels (the white colonel in command of the post) had the rebellious white officers and the enlisted men who refused to follow orders arrested and placed under guard by black sentries. As Gusley's comment suggests, the reports of this incident that circulated in the navy were highly critical of the result. As Commodore R. B. Hitchcock wrote several weeks later, "They are in a bad state at Ship Island. The n[egroes] have the upper hand, and have the poor whites under arrest." R. B. Hitchcock to T. A. Jenkins, Off Mobile, February 3, 1863, 19 ORN 599; C. P. Weaver, ed., *Thank God My Regiment an African One: The Civil War Diary of Colonel Nathan W. Daniels* (Baton Rouge: Louisiana State University Press, 1998), 26–29.

2. The word "moaks" was a derogatory term for black soldiers. It probably had its origin in the word "mocha," a type of coffee shipped from a port of that name at the entrance to the Red Sea. OED, 1826. The term would later also be applied derisively to the famous Buffalo Soldiers. Robert M. Utley, ed., *Life in Custer's Cavalry: Diaries and Letters of Albert and Jennie Barnitz*, (New Haven: Yale University Press, 1977), 99.

3. *Vincennes* was one of ten sloops-of-war authorized by Congress in 1825. Its crew was very experienced. Even before the Civil War, *Vincennes* had seen action in assignments varying from fighting pirates to global mapmaking and polar exploration. DANFS, 7:525–527.

4. As Gusley's journal confirms, in February 1863 a series of rumors reached the Navy that the Confederates were about to launch a fleet of ironclads to attack Ship Island. This same imaginary force was rumored to be preparing an attack on Pensacola and even New Orleans. Admiral Farragut did not believe there was truth in any of these rumors but as a precaution strengthened the naval presence in the area to deal with any potential attack that might develop. D. G. Farragut to H. A. Adams, New Orleans, February 4, 1863, 19 ORN 600.

5. Gusley's good opinion of General Rosecrans was perhaps due to the fact that the Union still maintained possession of the battlefield at Murfreesboro (Stone's River), Tennessee, on December 31, 1862, after a battle in which the Confederates probably achieved a tactical victory. Rosecrans would not stay in favor very long. After almost losing his entire army at the Battle of Chickamauga in September 1863, General Rosecrans was removed from command. Ezra J. Warner, *Generals in Blue* (Baton Rouge: Louisiana State University Press, 1964), 410–411.

6. Colonel Nathan W. Daniels, in command at Ship Island, recorded this event in his diary: "Washington's Birthday [I] ordered a salute of twenty-one guns to be fired which was done the grand old echoes reverberating for miles on the Gulf causing the secesh across the waters to wonder at our noise. The [Union fleet] all fired salutes and for a little while it looked like a real battle." Noting that *Clifton* actually fired its salute as it was headed out to sea to chase a blockade runner, Colonel Daniels observed that "it was a beautiful sight and awakened great enthusiasm both in the Army & Navy." Weaver, *Thank God My Regiment an African One*, 50–51.

7. This familiar saying is usually attributed to William Congreve's poem *The Mourning Bride* (1697).

8. Minstrel shows were the most popular form of shipboard entertainment. Some historians believe that they were designed to provide more than a simple diversion. Michael J. Bennett has observed that "for white sailors, these blackface productions both reaffirmed sailors' commonly held racial stereotypes and functioned as a public forum responsive to their racial and status insecurities in the postemancipation navy." Bennett, *Union Jacks*, 174.

9. "Skylarking" was the term used by sailors for a sort of organized free-for-all in which the men could do what-

ever they wanted, usually involving wrestling or fighting. It was a way of relieving tension. Skylarking was usually preceded by the boatswain's whistle piping "All hands to mischief!" Ibid., 116–117.

10. Richard L. Law, *Clifton*'s captain, was the subject of a court-martial proceeding because of the Union fleet's performance during the Battle of Galveston. As Nestell's cartoon of Law reflects, Law was chosen to be the official scapegoat for the Galveston debacle. In the resulting court-martial proceeding, Law was found guilty but his punishment was mitigated to sus-

pension from rank and duty for three years. General Order No. 28, Washington, D.C., January 7, 1864, 19 ORN 463–464.

11. This is the first line of William Cullen Bryant's poem *March* (1824).

12. The term "éclat" is a word of French derivation that was more commonly employed in Gusley's day. It means "brilliancy, radiance, or dazzling effect." OED, 830.

13. A "muggins" is a fool or simpleton. OED, 1871. In nineteenth-century popular literature it was common to have a character named Muggins who was the target of jokes and pranks.

## Chapter 13

1. The name Salathiel apparently refers to a romantic novel written in the 1820s by the Reverend George Croly, which identifies a man by that name as the legendary "wandering Jew," doomed to roam the earth until he witnesses the second coming of Christ. Also known as Shealtiel, Salathiel is identified in Matthew 1:12 as the father of Zerubbabel, one of the ancestors of Jesus.

2. Off the Mississippi coast south of Pascagoula, Round Island is one of the Mississippi barrier islands.

3. One provision in President Lincoln's Emancipation Proclamation addressed receiving slaves who came within Federal lines:

> And I further declare and make known that such persons of suitable condition will be received into the armed service of the United States to garrison forts, positions, stations, and other places, and to man vessels of all sorts in said service.

In practice this meant that many escaped slaves were assigned to perform some of the hardest and most disagreeable tasks on ships.

4. Grant's Pass was the western entrance into Mobile Bay from Mississippi Sound.

5. African Americans served in the naval forces in relatively large numbers.

Most historians estimate that between 15 and 20 percent of the men who served in the Union Navy were black. Bennett, *Union Jacks*, 12.

6. According to George Riddell, another Marine on *Clifton*, this captured blockade runner was one of the most successful in the area, having run the blockade twenty-seven times. Its owner, a man more than seventy years of age, was described as "one of the damnedest rascals in the South." The man boasted to his captors of his long career running slaves into the South. He also predicted that America would eventually degenerate into a monarchy. When warned that he was going to have to pay for his blockade violations, the old blockade runner scornfully replied to *Clifton*'s crew that "he done us as much harm as he could and now [that] you got me you can send me to hell if you like, I lived long enough." George Riddell to Brother John, Ship Island, March 21, 1863, Riddell Papers.

7. On March 14, 1863, Admiral Farragut tried to run his ships by the Confederate fortress at Port Hudson. One of his ships, *Mississippi*, ran aground. Unable to refloat it, the Union Navy was forced to blow *Mississippi* up to keep it out of Confederate hands. DANFS, 4:388.

## Chapter 14

1. This is a reference to Laurence Sterne's novel *A Sentimental Journey through France and Italy* (1768), in which a starling in a cage complains about its captivity, saying that it "can't get out."

2. In sailing terminology, this is a mode of tacking when the tide or current is with a vessel and the wind is against it. Under such conditions, little forward progress can be made and a ship essentially stands still.

3. *Clifton* was summoned to Louisiana because General Banks and his Army of the Gulf desperately needed shallow-draft gunboats to cooperate with their spring offensive up Bayou Teche. The purpose of this offensive was to cut the supply and communications lines to Port Hudson and enable Banks' force of infantry to cooperate with General Grant in operations against the Confederate strongholds at Port Hudson and Vicksburg. N. P. Banks to U. S. Grant, Brashear City, April 10, 1863, 15 OR 296; Donald S. Frazier, "Texans on the Teche: The Texas Brigade at the Battles of Bisland and Irish Bend, April 12–14, 1863," *Louisiana History* 32, no. 4 (fall 1991): 417–418.

4. The first Confederate conscription law, enacted in April 1862, applied to men between eighteen and thirty-five. Called by one historian "the first national military draft in U.S. history," it was revised in September 1862 to raise the maximum age to forty-five; five days later the legislators passed an expanded Exemption Act. Eventually, the Conscription Act of 1864 applied to all men between the ages of seventeen and fifty. Heidler and Heidler, *Encyclopedia of the Civil War*, 1:486 (entry on "Conscription, C.S.A.," by David Carlson).

5. Admiral Porter later described the danger of navigating in this complex country with the enemy hiding along the shores, saying, "No one who had not tried it could estimate the difficulties of ascending these Louisiana bayous and rivers. It was on these occasions (where men held their lives in their hands), that the most daring deeds of the war were performed." David D. Por-

ter, *The Naval History of the Civil War* (New York: Sherman, 1886), 277.

6. *Estrella* was a side-wheel steamer that had been transferred from the Army to the Navy in late 1862. In November 1862 and again in January 1863, *Estrella* had participated in a series of engagements with Confederate vessels and shore batteries along the Atchafalaya River and Bayou Teche. DANFS, 2:370–371.

7. *Diana* was a side-wheel steamer that had been captured by the Union at New Orleans when that city was seized in April 1862. On March 28, 1863, *Diana* was attacked and recaptured by the Confederates while on a reconnaissance mission on the Atchafalaya River and Grand Lake. DANFS, 2:275; Morris Raphael, *A Gunboat Named Diana* (Detroit: Harlo Press, 1993), 99–114.

8. Captain Thomas L. Peterson, whose body was recovered by the crew of *Calhoun* under a flag of truce, was reported to have been killed by a Minie ball through the heart. Acting Master's Mate Thomas G. Hall was killed by a similar shot through his lungs. Report of Fleet Surgeon J. M. Foltz, New Orleans, May 22, 1863, 20 ORN 110.

9. The town that Gusley refers to as Brashear City was originally known as Tigre Island because of the unusual cat by that name that had been spotted there by a group of early U.S. surveyors. As the area was settled, its rich resources and commercial potential attracted the attention of Kentucky planter and surgeon Walter Brashear. The subdivision of Brashear's sugarcane plantation led to the beginning of the town known at the time of the Civil War as Brashear. Following the war, Charles Morgan, a steamship and railroad entrepreneur, successfully dredged the Atchafalaya Bay Channel and made Brashear the center of his business operations. In 1876 the town was renamed Morgan City in his honor.

10. Gusley was more impressed with Brashear than many of the Union troops who garrisoned the place. Captain John De Forest of the Twelfth Connecticut wrote about Brashear: "The mosquitoes and other insects, including alligators, still form the largest part of

the native population, if not the worthiest." De Forest, *Volunteer's Adventures*, 154–155.

11. This was the Fourth Division of the Union's Army of the Gulf under the command of Brigadier-General Cuvier Grover. General Banks intended to march his main force up Bayou Teche from Berwick toward Confederate forces under General Richard Taylor at Bisland. In order to capture Taylor's force in its entirety, Banks planned for Grover and his force of eight thousand men to be transported up Grand Lake (by *Clifton* and other transports) to a position above Taylor's force where they could then march across the short distance to the Teche and cut off any Confederate retreat. Richard B. Irwin, *History of the Nineteenth Army Corps* (New York: G. P. Putnam's Sons, 1892), 104; Raphael, *Gunboat Named Diana*, 137.

12. "Chestimacha," or "Chetimaches," as it was labeled on some Union maps, was a general term referring collectively to Grand Lake, Flat Lake, Lake Pelourde, and other connected bodies of water in the area near Brashear City. Duganne, *Camps and Prisons*, 197.

13. This is a preliminary skirmish before the Battle of Irish Bend. Leaving Brashear City on the morning of April 12, 1863, *Clifton* transported Grover's division of the Nineteenth Corps up Grand Lake to a point near Charenton and the bend in the Teche called Indian Bend. This was an attempt to cut off the retreat of Confederate forces from Fort Bisland. At about 6 A.M. the next day, elements of the U.S. First Louisiana Volunteers were landing when enemy artillery and sharpshooters opened fire. Within twenty minutes *Clifton's* heavy guns forced the Confederates from their position and silenced their guns. J. L. Hallett to G. R. Her-

bert, Port Hudson, July 10, 1863, 15 OR 363; Raphael, *Gunboat Named Diana*, 140–141.

14. One Connecticut soldier later observed, "The Teche country was to the war in Louisiana what the Shenandoah Valley was to the war in Virginia. It was a sort of back alley, parallel to the main street wherein the heavy fighting must go on; and one side or the other was always running up or down the Teche with the other side in full chase after it." De Forest, *Volunteer's Adventures*, 85.

15. At about 4 P.M. on April 13, 1863, *Clifton* arrived about three miles below Camp Bisland, where it found the Teche obstructed with "torpedoes" (mines). To let the Union Army know it was there, *Clifton* sent a shell from its nine-inch gun to explode above the Confederate fort. Removing the mines took until 10 A.M. the next day, when *Clifton* finally proceeded up the Teche to Fort Bisland. As a signalman from the Twenty-eighth Maine regiment assigned to *Clifton* recorded, "we took an active part in the fight that was then going on at Camp Bisland, our shot and shell having excellent effect on their works." T. S. Hall to G. R. Herbert, Port Hudson, July 16, 1863, 15 OR 364; Irwin, *History of the Nineteenth Army Corps*, 100–102.

16. At dawn on April 14, the Union gunboats *Estrella*, *Calhoun*, and *Arizona* saw a large black steamer approaching them on Grand Lake. The three ships opened fire with their rifled guns at the steamer, which turned out to be C.S.S. *Queen of the West*. Within twenty minutes the Union bombardment had set *Queen of the West* on fire and destroyed it. A. P. Cooke to H. W. Morris, Grand Lake, April 15, 1863, 20 ORN 134–135.

## Chapter 15

1. Erected in late 1862, this fort (also called Fort Butte a la Rose) was located strategically at the western end of Cow Island at the place where Cow Island Bayou, the Atchafalaya River, and Bayou a la Rose meet. Roberts, *Encyclopedia of Historic Forts*, 333. The fort had only two old siege guns, one 24-pounder and

one 32-pounder. A. P. Cooke to H. Morris, Butte a la Rose, April 22, 1863, 20 ORN 153.

2. Joining *Clifton* in this attack were the gunboats *Arizona*, *Calhoun*, and *Estrella*. They reached the Confederate fort at about 10 A.M. For a period of about thirty minutes, one observer

recorded, "shell and shot did rain . . . in earnest." Finally, after the gunboats resorted to firing grapeshot to drive the Confederates from their guns, "the Bars and Stars were down and a white flag in their place." Letter from "Young Neptune" on board U.S.S. *Arizona*, *(Toledo) Daily Commercial*, May 8, 1863. As one engineer described the "short, sharp and decisive" attack, "It was done after the style of Daddy Farragut: we rush in." Diary of Engineer George W. Baird, April 20, 1863, 20 ORN 154. Lieutenant Robert Rhodes of *Clifton* wrote later, "Our men stood at their guns and fought them with great bravery. It was a trying time to both officers and men when our guns became muzzle to muzzle with those of the rebels. But when they dashed up to the fort they sent up tremendous cheers." Bartlett, *Memoirs of Rhode Island Officers*, 301–302 (statement of Robert Rhodes). Heavily damaged in the brief attack, *Clifton* was awarded the captured fort's flag after the battle. A. P. Cooke to F. Crocker, On Gunboat *Estrella*, April 21, 1863, 20 ORN 155.

3. The Confederate cottonclad gunboat that evaded capture on this occasion was *J. A. Cotton (II)*, formerly named *Mary T*. Because it replaced an earlier Confederate ship by the same name, it was sometimes known as *Cotton Jr.*; A. P. Cooke to H. W. Morris, Butte-a-la-Rose, April 22, 1863, 20 ORN 153–154; Silverstone, *Civil War Navies*, 187.

4. Gusley's Note-Book entry makes it sound as though these supplies were finding their own way into Federal hands. Actually, the Union armed forces were active participants in the liberation of these supplies. On *Arizona*, the sailors were more candid about this bounty, with one man writing home to Ohio, "On our way back to [Fort

Burton], we went on shore at the plantations and foraged to our hearts' delight among the cattle, sheep, turkeys and chickens, etc." Letter from "Young Neptune," *(Toledo) Daily Commercial*, May 8, 1863.

5. The escaped slaves were not treated as honored refugees. As one sailor described the result, "Thousands of contrabands are running away and following the armies; everybody have as many servants as they please." Letter from "Young Neptune," *(Toledo) Daily Commercial*, July 14, 1863.

6. On April 7, 1863, a large force of ironclads under the command of Samuel Du Pont tried to enter Charleston Harbor and capture the city. The Confederate batteries inflicted substantial damage to the ironclads and, as Gusley recorded, the Union fleet was forced to withdraw. S. F. Du Pont to G. Welles, Port Royal Harbor, April 15, 1863, 14 ORN 5–8.

7. Admiral David Porter successfully passed the Confederate guns at Fort De Russy and unexpectedly encountered no resistance when he arrived at Alexandria. D. Porter to G. Welles, Alexandria, May 7, 1863, 24 ORN 645.

8. Mortimer Thompson (1832–1875) was an American journalist and humorist who wrote under the pseudonym Q. K. Philander Doesticks. A staff writer for the *New York Tribune*, his poetry and stories, especially those expressing antislavery sentiments, attracted wide attention. During the Civil War he served as a war correspondent for the *Tribune* and also as chaplain to a Union regiment. His best-known works include *Doesticks: What He Says* (1855).

9. To "cheer ship" was to give a formal salute through the cheers of sailors stationed in the rigging.

## Chapter 16

1. Gusley was not alone in his skepticism about the effectiveness of the Mobile blockade. Admiral Farragut lamented in late May 1863, "I am constantly in receipt of letters from Havana announcing arrivals there of vessels from Mobile and its vicinity."

D. Farragut to J. R. Goldsborough, New Orleans, May 21, 1863, 20 ORN 205.

2. On April 12, 1863, Acting Master George C. Andrews and a party of fourteen Confederates from Mobile captured the Union transport *Fox* near the mouth of the Mississippi and took it into Mobile with its entire crew of

twenty-three men as prisoners. Extract from Report of the Secretary of the Navy, undated, 20 ORN 809.

3. Although Gusley did not know it, Vicksburg surrendered on July 4, 1863, only a week after he wrote this entry in his Note-Book.

4. Once again, the news that Gusley received was old and erroneous. Although General Robert E. Lee had indeed invaded Pennsylvania, by the time that Gusley wrote this entry, Lee had already lost the Battle of Gettysburg. In fact, Lee was beginning to retreat from Gusley's home state almost as the young marine learned of the beginning of Lee's Pennsylvania campaign.

5. Port Hudson surrendered on July 9, 1863.

6. Like Round Island, Horn Island is another of Mississippi's barrier islands. It is a long, crescent-shaped island almost due south of Pascagoula and Round Island.

7. This is probably a paraphrase of verse 4:16 of the Song of Solomon: "Awake, O north wind; come, O south wind! Blow on my garden so that its fragrant spices may send out their sweet smell."

8. One of the ships captured during this expedition was the barge *H. McGuin* of New Orleans, which was allegedly engaged in trading with the enemy at the time of its seizure. H. A. Adams Jr. to G. Welles, Ship Island, July 18, 1863, 20 ORN 399.

## Chapter 17

1. *Hollyhock* was a side-wheel tug that had been captured in the Bahama Channel in July 1862. It was purchased by the U.S. government in March 1863 and was used as a lightly armed tender and supply ship for the rest of the war. Silverstone, *Civil War Navies*, 85.

2. Captain Crocker reported that near Camp Bisland, *Clifton* "encountered Sibley's Brigade, or a portion of it, with Haldeman's battery of six pieces, all of whom I drove into the works of that place and then shelled them out again, causing them to retreat rapidly beyond the range of my guns." F. Crocker to H. W. Morris, Off Brashear City, July 28, 1863, 20 ORN 380.

3. Union forces arrived at Brashear City beginning on July 22, 1863, and entered the city without opposition. Although the docks and landings were undamaged, the railroad tracks were torn up and were obstructed by the ruins of fifty-two burned railroad cars and two engines. F. H. Peck to R. B. Irwin, Brashear City, July 25, 1863, 20 ORN 379.

4. The policy of the Union Navy toward escaped black slaves was the source of a great deal of confusion in the Gulf of Mexico. In May 1863, Washington announced that "the large number of persons known as contrabands flocking to the protection of the United States flag affords an opportunity to provide in every department of a ship, especially for boats' crews, acclimated labor." Flag-officers were instructed to enlist them freely in the navy. General Order of Rear-Admiral D. G. Farragut, Off Baton Rouge, May 9, 1863, 20 ORN 174. At the end of June, Secretary of the Navy Gideon Welles called Admiral Farragut's attention to newspaper reports that near Brashear City there were more than seven thousand black people being fed at government expense, and inquired whether some of the able-bodied men could be enlisted for naval service. G. Welles to D. G. Farragut, Navy Department, June 27, 1863, 20 ORN 322. As Gusley's comment suggests, however, so many black men were subsequently taken aboard naval ships in response to these policies that the sailors began to resent them, causing such bad treatment that some of the escaped slaves deserted from naval service. D. G. Farragut to G. Welles, New Orleans, July 16, 1863, 20 ORN 395–396; Bennett, *Union Jacks*, 159–162.

5. This saying probably was based on the Irish custom of giving a "marriage bell" to a newly married couple. The bell was intended to be used when one of the parties to the marriage wished to end a dispute. Either party could ring the bell. Ringing the bell was supposed to remind the spouses of their wedding bells and smooth over the argument.

6. "All quiet along the line" became a

common saying following publication of "All Quiet Along the Potomac To-night," a popular poem written by Ethel Lynn Beers that first appeared under the title "The Picket Guard" in *Harper's Weekly Magazine* on November 30, 1861.

7. Louisiana was the largest sugar producer in the South. Sugar mills and associated extraction and storage facilities were combined into structures (usually brick) known as "sugar houses." These sugar houses made convenient targets for Union naval gunners because they were typically located near the water, the main route by which the sugar had been exported to market before the war. One Louisiana girl complained in her diary of the continual noise of Union gunners "banging away at some treasonable sugar houses that are disobedient enough to grind cane on the other side of the river." Sarah Morgan Dawson, *A Confederate Girl's Diary* (Bloomington: Indiana University Press, 1960), 289.

8. "Cast loose and provide" or "cast off and provide" was one of the first of a series of commands used to get naval guns into position and equipped so they could be fired. Coggins, *Arms and Equipment of the Civil War*, 144.

9. A "sawyer" is an American term for a tree swept into a river that usually has one end stuck in the mud, leaving the other end to bob up and down, forming

a hazard to ships attempting to navigate the river.

10. A "bower" is an anchor that was mounted near the bow of a vessel. OED, 258.

11. This is the beginning of the expedition to invade Texas through Sabine Pass. To fool spies as to the expedition's real destination, General Nathaniel Banks stationed pilots from Mobile on board the ships as they headed down the Mississippi River to lend the impression that the ships were headed east rather than west when they reached the Gulf of Mexico.

12. Located at the border between Texas and Louisiana, Sabine Pass was the passage to the Gulf of Mexico of waters from a vast drainage area that included much of eastern Texas and western Louisiana. This was a popular port for blockade runners and was a very important point for Texas Confederates to import arms and military supplies. Cotham, *Sabine Pass*, 9–16.

13. Organized primarily from Seneca and Cayuga Counties, New York, this regiment had seen a wide range of action in Florida and Louisiana. They had participated actively in the Teche campaigns and assaults against Port Hudson. Henry Hall and James Hall, *Cayuga in the Field* (Auburn, New York: Truair, Smith & Co., 1873), 97.

## Chapter 18

1. General Banks estimated the size of the Army's force at approximately five thousand men. N. P. Banks to H. W. Halleck, New Orleans, September 5, 1863, 26 OR [Part 1] 286.

2. The phrase "hammer and tongs" means to go at something after the fashion of a blacksmith, raining a series of loud, rapid blows. OED, 1247.

3. The identity of Gusley's exception is uncertain. Captain Crocker listed

two possible candidates in his official battle report. Acting Master Benjamin S. Weeks hauled down the flag to surrender *Clifton* without Crocker's permission. Crocker long after the battle also complained of the conduct of his surgeon, Dr. Daniel Nestell, who hid on the ship's rudder chain during part of the battle. Report of F. Crocker, Edgartown, Massachusetts, April 21, 1865, 20 ORN 547.

## Chapter 19

1. Published in the *Galveston Tri-Weekly News* on October 10, 1863, this letter was written from prison by Henry O. Gusley.

According to John Read, a naval officer who was confined there along with Gusley, "Camp Groce, near the town of Hempstead, was an enclosure surrounded by a stockade about fifteen feet in height, made by piles driven into the ground, on the top of which at intervals of about fifty feet were sentry boxes of the guards. Inside the pen was one old barrack, not sufficient, however, for all the prisoners, and but little protection from the weather, as all boards were off on roof and sides. Several thousand prisoners in all were confined here." John Read, "Texas Prisons and a Comparison of Northern and Southern Prison Camps," in *Military Order of the Loyal Legion of the United States (New York Commandery)*, Vol. 4 (1912; reprinted, Wilmington, North Carolina: Broadfoot Publishing, 1992), 23:254.

Born in Marblehead, Massachusetts, in 1802, Willard Richardson moved to Texas in 1837 to work initially as a surveyor. Discarding that profession in 1841, he started a boys school in Houston. Three years later, he filled in as temporary editor for a local newspaper and showed such promise that he was hired for the same position by the *Galveston News*. At the *News*, Richardson earned the reputation of being the "Napoleon of the Texas Press" because of his aggressive style. He was an ardent supporter of the institution of slavery, a vigorous proponent of secession, and a defender of the doctrine of states' rights. Tyler, *New Handbook of Texas*, 5:572 (entry on "Richardson, Willard," by Randolph Lewis).

2. Published in the *Galveston Tri-Weekly News* on October 31, 1863, this letter was also written by Henry O. Gusley.

3. William Shakespeare, *Hamlet*, 3.1.

# Index